THE COMPACT CATHOLIC PRAYER BOOK

Compiled by the editors
of The Word Among Us Press

Copyright © 2008 The Word Among Us Press
Updated Edition © 2011
All rights reserved
7115 Guilford Drive
Frederick, Maryland 21704
www.wau.org

19 18 17 16 15   5 6 7 8 9

ISBN: 978-1-59325-127-7

Made and printed in the United States of America
Cover design by John Hamilton Design

Acknowledgments on page 6.

Library of Congress Cataloging-in-Publication Data
The compact Catholic prayer book / compiled by the editors of The
Word Among Us Press.
    p. cm.
  ISBN 978-1-59325-127-7 (alk. paper)
  1. Catholic Church--Prayers and devotions. I. Word Among Us
Press.
  BX2149.2.C66 2008
  242'.802--dc22
                              2007040537

Acquire the habit of speaking to God as if you were alone with him. Speak with familiarity and confidence as to your dearest and most loving friend. Speak of your life, your plans, your troubles, your joys, your fears. In return, God will speak to you—not that you will hear audible words in your ears, but words that you will clearly understand in your heart.

—St. Alphonsus Liguori (1696–1787)

CONTENTS

ACKNOWLEDGMENTS

We thank Evelyn Bence for her research and compilation assistance, and she thanks John Breslin, SJ, for his encouragement and library help one crisp autumn day. Thanks also to Bob French, who used his experience and talent to write many of the prayers in Part 5.

The English translation of the Apostles' Creed, the Nicene Creed, the *Confiteor,* and Eucharistic Prayers I, II, III, and IV from *The Roman Missal* © 2010, International Commission on English in the Liturgy Corporation (ICEL); the English translation of the Act of Contrition (contemporary version) from *Rite of Penance* © 1974, ICEL. All rights reserved.

Contemporary English translations of the *Benedictus, Gloria Patri,* the Hail Mary, the Lord's Prayer, the *Magnificat, Nunc Dimittus,* and *Te Deum* © 1989, International Consultation on English Texts. All rights reserved. Used with permission.

Unless otherwise noted, Scripture passages are from the New Revised Standard Version Bible: Catholic Edition, copyright © 1989, 1993 Division of Christian Education of the National Council of the Churches of Christ in the United States. All rights reserved. Used with permission.

Scripture citations from the New Jerusalem Bible, copyright © 1985 by Darton, Longman, & Todd, Ltd., and Doubleday, a division of Bantam Doubleday Dell Publishing Group, Inc. Reprinted by permission.

INTRODUCTION

COME, SEEK GOD'S FACE. DRAW NEAR TO GOD'S HEART

*Hear, O L*ord*, when I cry aloud,*
be gracious to me and answer me!
"Come," my heart says, "seek his face!"
*Your face, L*ord*, do I seek.*
Do not hide your face from me.

—Psalm 27:7-9

The Catholic Church has always valued two kinds of prayer: the communal prayer of believers gathered together for worship and the celebration of the Eucharist, and the personal prayer of individuals, communicating with God privately and devotionally. The prayers selected in this book honor and recognize both of these traditions. This is a book that you can take to church to allow you to follow along during the Eucharistic Prayer or to focus your attention on the Blessed Sacrament. It is also a book to keep at your bedside or in your purse or briefcase to help you structure a personal prayer time.

Many of the prayers in the following pages have been handed down by Christians from generation to generation. Some of the prayers presented as poems were traditionally sung as hymns of praise. We've chosen a few biblical prayers, principally psalms, and also prayers written by saints, many of them asking for gifts and graces to strengthen us spiritually on a journey toward holiness. Some traditionally communal prayers are longer, such as the Eucharistic Prayer itself (in part 2), the Rosary and the Litany of the Saints (in part 3), and the Stations of the Cross (in part 4). Many of the prayers in the last section have been written by Bob French, a contributor to *The Word Among Us* magazine, expressly for this volume.

Of course, speaking to God, whether giving praise or seeking grace, is only part of the dynamic of Christian prayer. Prayer also involves listening. Jesus, the apostles, and the saints knew the voice of the Holy Spirit, speaking heart to heart. And the Spirit still directs, nudges, and consoles us as we quiet our minds and listen—communication beyond the words printed in these pages.

With this invitation to prayer, we also offer a word of encouragement to those who may have first opened this book with the sincere intention to pray regularly—maybe fervently and formally—but who lost the discipline of a scheduled routine. We suggest that you make a fresh start by finding a place and identifying a time when you can faithfully and comfortably pray. And we encourage you with the words of St. Irenaeus (c. 130–c. 200), one of the early fathers of the church. "Patience and perseverance are never more thoroughly Christian graces than when they are features of prayer." His challenge to persevere is linked to patience. Patience with God but also patience with ourselves, to turn again and again toward the face of our Lord, Jesus Christ.

PART 1

EVERYDAY PRAYERS

Why should you fear or be ashamed when
armed with the sign of the cross?
—St. Augustine (354–430)

For centuries Catholics have learned a number of foundational prayers that have grounded their daily devotional life. They are so universal that some are known by familiar short-form names: the Sign of the Cross, the Glory Be, the Our Father, the Hail Mary, the Act of Faith . . . Hope . . . Love.

These basic prayers lead us to other everyday prayers, first those asking for daily blessing, followed by those that invoke the Lord's presence or ask the Holy Spirit to come and make himself known in a special way.

From the ancient psalms, we learn the powerful prayer dynamic of praise. We end this "everyday" section with what we've called "prayers on the run." Traditionally such one-sentence prayers were called ejaculations—short cries for help or thanksgiving that serve to remind us that God hears our informal prayers as well as our formal intercessions.

Chapter 1 | FOUNDATIONAL PRAYERS

The Sign of the Cross

An ancient prayer of personal blessing that combines physical gestures with the Trinitarian names of God:

In the name of the Father (touching the forehead),
and of the Son (touching the heart),
and of the Holy Spirit (touching the left and then right
    shoulders). Amen.

Apostles' Creed

I believe in God,
the Father almighty,
Creator of heaven and earth,
and in Jesus Christ, his only Son, our Lord,
who was conceived by the Holy Spirit,
born of the Virgin Mary,
suffered under Pontius Pilate,
was crucified, died and was buried;
he descended into hell;
on the third day he rose again from the dead;

he ascended into heaven,
and is seated at the right hand of God the Father
    almighty;
from there he will come to judge the living and the dead.

I believe in the Holy Spirit,
the holy catholic Church,
the communion of saints,
the forgiveness of sins,
the resurrection of the body,
and life everlasting. Amen.

Our Father: The Lord's Prayer
Traditional Version

Our Father, who art in heaven,
hallowed be thy name;
thy kingdom come,
thy will be done
on earth as it is in heaven.
Give us this day our daily bread,
and forgive us our trespasses,
as we forgive those who trespass against us;
and lead us not into temptation,
but deliver us from evil. Amen.

Our Father: The Lord's Prayer
Contemporary Version

Our Father in heaven,
  hallowed be your name,
  your kingdom come,
  your will be done,
  on earth as in heaven.
Give us today our daily bread.
Forgive us our sins
  as we forgive those who sin against us.
Save us from the time of trial
  and deliver us from evil.
For the kingdom, the power, and the glory are yours,
  now and forever. Amen.

Hail Mary

Hail Mary, full of grace,
the Lord is with you!
Blessed are you among women,
and blessed is the fruit of your womb, Jesus.
Holy Mary, Mother of God,
pray for us sinners,
now and at the hour of our death. Amen.

Glory Be: Gloria Patri
Traditional Version

Glory be to the Father
and to the Son
and to the Holy Spirit.
As it was in the beginning,
is now and ever shall be—
world without end. Amen.

Glory Be: Gloria Patri
Contemporary Version

Glory to the Father
and to the Son
and to the Holy Spirit:
as it was in the beginning,
is now, and will be forever. Amen.

Prayer to the Holy Spirit

Come, Holy Spirit, fill the hearts of your faithful
    and enkindle in them the fire of your love.
Send forth your Spirit and they shall be created,
    and you shall renew the face of the earth.

Let us pray: O God, who by the light of the Holy Spirit instructs the hearts of the faithful, grant that by the same Spirit we may be truly wise and ever rejoice in his consolation, through Christ our Lord. Amen.

Prayer Before the Acts of Faith, Hope, and Love

Give me, O God, an increase of faith, hope, and charity. To obtain what you promised, grant that I may love and practice what you command, through Jesus Christ, my Lord. Amen.

Act of Faith

O my God, I firmly believe in one God, in three divine persons: the Father, the Son, and the Holy Spirit. I believe in Jesus Christ, the true and only Son of God, who was born of the virgin Mary, and died on the cross for our salvation. I also believe all the sacred truths the Catholic Church believes and teaches, because you, who can neither deceive nor be deceived, have revealed them. In this faith I desire to live. And in the same faith, by your holy grace, I am resolved to die. Amen.

Act of Hope

O my God, relying on your almighty power, confiding in your infinite goodness and mercy, and in your sacred promises, I hope to receive pardon of all my sins, and grace to serve you faithfully in this life, and life everlasting, through the merits of Jesus Christ, my Lord and Savior. Amen.

Act of Love

O my God, I love you above all things, with my whole heart and soul, because you are infinitely worthy of love. Out of love for you, I love also my neighbor as myself. I forgive all who have injured me and ask pardon for all whom I have injured. Amen.

Chapter 2 | DAILY BLESSINGS: MORNING, NOON, AND NIGHT

A Morning Offering

O Jesus, through the Immaculate Heart of Mary, I offer you my prayers, works, joys, and sufferings of this day, in union with the holy sacrifice of the Mass throughout the world. I offer them for all the intentions of your sacred heart: the salvation of souls, reparation for sin, and the reunion of all Christians. I offer them for the intentions of our bishops and in particular for those recommended by our Holy Father. Amen.

(For specific monthly intentions of the Holy Father, contact the Apostleship of Prayer in the United States at www.apostleshipofprayer.org.)

Morning Prayers

O my God! I adore and love you with all my heart. I thank you for the many favors and benefits I have received from your infinite goodness and mercy, especially for having preserved me last night.

O my God! I am sorry for having offended you; grant that I may spend this day well. Grant me your holy blessing and the grace to avoid serious sin.

O my God! I offer all my actions today to you. I pray that whatever I do may be acceptable to you; give me grace to do all to your honor and glory.

O holy Mary! I put myself under your protection and beg the help of your prayers.

O my good angel! Be also my protector and pray to God for me, that I may do his holy will in all things. Amen.

O Lord God Almighty, who has brought us to the beginning of this day, defend us by your power, that we may not fall into any sin, but that all our thoughts, words, and actions may be directed to the fulfillment of your will. Through Jesus Christ our Lord. Amen.

O Lord God, King of heaven and earth, direct and sanctify us this day. Rule and govern our hearts and bodies, our thoughts, words, and actions according to your commandments, that now and ever we may by your help attain salvation and freedom, O Savior of the world, who lives and reigns for ever and ever. Amen.

Benedictus
(Canticle of Zechariah, Luke 1:68-79)

Blessed be the Lord, the God of Israel;
he has come to his people and set them free.

He has raised up for us a mighty savior,
born of the house of his servant David.

Through his holy prophets he promised of old
    that he would save us from our enemies,
    from the hands of all who hate us.

He promised to show mercy to our fathers
and to remember his holy covenant.

This was the oath that he swore to our father Abraham:
to set us free from the hands of our enemies,
free to worship him without fear,
holy and righteous in his sight all the days of our life.

You, my child, shall be called the prophet of the
    Most High;
for you will go before the Lord to prepare his way,

to give his people knowledge of salvation
by the forgiveness of their sins.
In the tender compassion of our God
the dawn from on high shall break upon us,
to shine on those who dwell in darkness and the shadow
    of death,
and to guide our feet into the way of peace.

Glory to the Father, and to the Son,
    and to the Holy Spirit:
as it was in the beginning, is now,
    and will be for ever. Amen.

Your Will Be Done Today
Thomas à Kempis (1380–1471)

O Lord, you know what is best for me. Let me conduct myself according to your pleasure. Give what you will, how much you will, and when you will. Set me where you will and deal with me as you think best. Behold, I am your servant, prepared for anything, for I desire not to live for myself but for you. May I do so worthily and perfectly. Amen.

Daily Prayer Before the Image of Jesus
St. Thomas Aquinas (c. 1225–c. 1275)

Grant me grace, O merciful God, to desire all that is pleasing to you, to examine it prudently, to acknowledge it truthfully, and to accomplish it perfectly, for the praise and glory of your name. Amen.

All My Days
Elizabeth Barrett Browning (1806–1861)

I praise thee while my days go on.
I love thee while my days go on.
Through dark and dearth, through fire and frost,
With emptied arms and treasure lost,
I thank thee while my days go on. Amen.

Support Us All the Day Long
John Henry Newman (1801–1890)

O Lord, support us all the day long of this troubled life,
until the shadows lengthen,
and the evening comes,
and the busy world is hushed,

and the fever of life is over,
and our work is done.
Then of your mercy
grant us a safe lodging,
and a holy rest,
and peace at the last,
    through Jesus Christ our Lord. Amen.

Grace Before Meals

Bless us, Lord, and these your gifts
which we are about to receive from your goodness.
Through Christ our Lord. Amen.

Heavenly Father, great and good,
We thank you for this daily food.
Bless us even as we pray.
Guide and keep us through the day. Amen.

Grace After Meals

Father, make us thankful for all your blessings. Be with
us today and sustain us for your service, in the name of
our blessed Redeemer. Amen.

We give thanks for all your gifts, Almighty God,
living and reigning now and for ever. Amen.

An Evening Prayer

O most gracious God, I offer to you my sleep and
watching, in union with all the sleep and watching of your
Son my Savior and also with his resurrection. After three
days, he awoke from death, as it were from sleep, and by
his own power took his life again.

Grant that I may so use the necessary rest of my body
and so employ my waking hours that all may tend to
your greater glory and the salvation of my soul. Amen.

An Evening Hymn
Thomas Ken (1637–1711)

All praise to you, my God, this night,
for all the blessings of the light:
keep me, O keep me, King of Kings,
beneath your own almighty wings.

Forgive me, Lord, for your dear Son,
the ill that I this day have done;

that with the world, myself, and thee,
I, while I sleep, at peace may be.

O may my soul on you repose,
and with sweet sleep my eyelids close;
sleep that shall me more vigorous make
to serve my God when I awake. Amen.

A Night Prayer
St. Alphonsus Liguori (1696–1787)

Jesus Christ, my God, I adore you, and I thank you for all the graces you have granted me this day. I offer to you my sleep and every moment of this night. I place myself within your sacred side and under the protecting mantle of Our Lady, my mother. May your holy angels help me and keep me in peace, and may your blessing be upon me. Amen.

Nunc Dimittis
(The Song of Simeon, Luke 2:29-32)

Lord, now let your servant go in peace;
your word has been fulfilled:

my own eyes have seen the salvation
which you have prepared in the sight of every people:

a light to reveal you to the nations
and the glory of your people Israel.

Chapter 3 | PRAYERS TO THE FATHER, SON, AND HOLY SPIRIT

Ephesians 3:14-21

I bow my knees before the Father, from whom every family in heaven and on earth takes its name. I pray that, according to the riches of his glory, he may grant that you may be strengthened in your inner being with power through his Spirit, and that Christ may dwell in your hearts through faith, as you are being rooted and grounded in love. I pray that you may have the power to comprehend, with all the saints, what is the breadth and length and height and depth, and to know the love of Christ that surpasses knowledge, so that you may be filled with all the fullness of God.

Now to him who by the power at work within us is able to accomplish abundantly far more than all we can ask or imagine, to him be glory in the church and in Christ Jesus to all generations, forever and ever. Amen.

God Be in My Head
From the Sarum Primer (1558)

God be in my head, and in my understanding.
God be in my eyes, and in my looking.
God be in my mouth, and in my speaking.
God be in my heart, and in my thinking.
God be at my end, and at my departing.

The Jesus Prayer

The apostle Paul tells us to "Pray without ceasing" (1 Thessalonians 5:17). For centuries, this concise prayer has been the constant heart-cry of Christians acknowledging the lordship of Jesus, the power of his name, and their own depravity and need. Typically people say the prayer repetitively as a focus for meditation and as an impetus for contemplation. The prayer is based on models found in the gospel: Luke 18:13, 38.

Lord Jesus Christ, Son of the living God, have mercy on me, a sinner.

Come, O Jesus

Blessed Mary of the Angels (1661–1717)

Come, O King of Heaven, prepare my heart by purifying my conscience, that I may worthily go to meet you.

Come, O God of Hosts, to bless me and give me your peace, and all my soul will be in peace.

Come, Eternal Wisdom, instruct me in holy fear, and teach me the way to heaven.

O Good Shepherd, come and seek for the wandering sheep and save it.

You are our Lawgiver: come and impress on my heart the love of your holy precepts.

You are the King of nations: come and reign over all my affections.

You are the King of Israel: come and take complete possession of my heart.

You are the Key of David: come and open to me the treasures of your mercy.

You are the splendor of the glory of the Father: come and display to my eyes the radiance of your virtues.

In a word, descend O divine Word, from the bosom of the Eternal Father to the womb of Mary, and from the bosom of Mary come—ah come!—into my soul. Amen.

O Jesus, Living in Mary
St. Louis de Montfort (1673–1716)

O Jesus, living in Mary!
come and live in your servant,
in the spirit of your sanctity,
in the fullness of your power,
in the perfection of your ways,
in the truth of your virtues,
and in the communion of your mysteries.
Triumph over all adverse powers,
in your Holy Spirit, for the glory of your Father. Amen.

St. Patrick's Breastplate
St. Patrick (389–461)

I bind unto myself today
the strong name of the Trinity,
by invocation of the same,
the Three in One, and One in Three.
By whom all nature has creation,
eternal Father, Spirit, Word:
praise to the Lord of my salvation,
salvation is of Christ the Lord.

I bind this day to me forever,
by power of faith, Christ's incarnation;
his baptism in the Jordan River;
his death on the cross for my salvation;
his bursting from the spiced tomb;
his riding up the heavenly way;
his coming at the day of doom:
I bind unto myself today.

Christ be with me,
Christ within me,
Christ behind me,
Christ before me,
Christ beside me,
Christ to win me,
Christ to comfort and restore me,
Christ beneath me,
Christ above me,
Christ in quiet,
Christ in danger,
Christ in hearts of all that love me,
Christ in mouth of friend and stranger.

Lord Jesus, Think on Me

Synesius of Cyrene (c. 373–c. 414)

Lord Jesus, think on me
and purge away my sin;
From earthborn passions set me free,
and make me pure within.

Lord Jesus, think on me,
with care and woe oppressed;
Let me your loving servant be,
and taste your promised rest.
Lord Jesus, think on me,
don't let me go astray;
Through darkness and perplexity,
show me the heavenly way.

Lord Jesus, think on me,
that when the flood is past,
I may the eternal brightness see,
and share your joy at last.

Breathe in Me, O Holy Spirit
St. Augustine (354–430)

Breathe in me, O Holy Spirit,
that my thoughts may all be holy.
Act in me, O Holy Spirit,
that my work, too, may be holy.
Draw my heart, O Holy Spirit,
that I may love only what is holy.
Strengthen me, O Holy Spirit,
that I may defend all that is holy.
Guard me, then, O Holy Spirit,
that I always may be holy. Amen.

Come, Holy Spirit
(Veni Sancte Spiritus)

Come, O Holy Spirit, come!
and from your celestial home
shed a ray of light divine.
Come, O Father of the poor.
Come, O Source of all our store.
Come, within our spirits shine.

You, of comforters the best;
you, the soul's most welcome guest:
sweet refreshment here below.
In our labor, rest most sweet;
grateful coolness in the heat;
solace in the midst of woe.

O most blessed light divine,
shine within these hearts of thine,
and our inmost being fill.
Where you are not, man has naught,
nothing good in deed or thought,
nothing free from taint of ill.

Heal our wounds, our strength renew;
on our dryness pour your dew;
wash the stains of guilt away:
Bend the stubborn heart and will,
melt the frozen, warm the chill;
guide the steps that go astray.

On the faithful, who adore
and confess you, evermore
in your sevenfold gifts descend;

give them virtue's sure reward;
give them your salvation, Lord;
give them joys that never end.

Come, Creator Spirit, Come
(Veni Creator Spiritus)

O come, Creator Spirit, come,
from your bright, heavenly throne;
come, take possession of our souls,
and make them all your own.

You who are called the Paraclete,
best gift of God above;
the living spring, the vital fire,
sweet christ'ning and true love.

You who are sevenfold in your grace,
finger of God's right hand;
his promise, teaching little ones
to speak and understand.

O guide our minds with your blest light,
with love our hearts inflame;

and with your strength, which never decays,
confirm our mortal frame.

Drive far from us our deadly foe,
true peace unto us bring;
and through all perils lead us safe,
beneath your sacred wing.

Through you may we the Father know;
through you the eternal Son,
and you, the Spirit of them both:
O blessed Three in One.

All glory to the Father be,
and to his risen Son,
the same to you, great Paraclete,
while endless ages run.

Chapter 4 | PRAYERS OF PRAISE

The Canticle of Brother Sun
(Praises of the Creatures)
St. Francis of Assisi (1181–1226)

Most high, omnipotent, good Lord,
yours be the praise, the glory, the honor, and benediction.
To you alone, Most High, they are due,
and no man is worthy to mention you.

Be praised, my Lord, by all your creatures,
above all by brother sun, who gives the day and lightens
    us therewith.
And he is beautiful and radiant with great splendor,
of you, Most High, he bears similitude.

Be praised, my Lord, by sister moon and the stars,
in the heaven you have formed them, clear and precious
    and comely.
Be praised, my Lord, by brother wind,
and of the air, and the cloud, and of fair and of all
    weather,
by which you give to your creatures sustenance.

Be praised, my Lord, by sister water,
which is much useful and humble and precious and pure.

Be praised, my Lord, by brother fire,
by which you have lightened the night,
and he is beautiful and joyful and robust and strong.

Be praised, my Lord, by our sister mother earth,
which sustains and rules us,
and produces many different fruits and colored flowers
    and herbs.

Be praised, my Lord, by those who show pardon by
        your love
and endure sickness and tribulations.
Blessed are they who will endure it in peace,
for by you, Most High, they shall be crowned.

Be praised, my Lord, by our sister bodily death,
from whom no one living may escape;
woe to those who die in mortal sin.
Blessed are they who are found in your most holy will,
for the second death shall not work them ill.

Praise and bless my Lord, and give him thanks,
and serve him with great humility. Amen.

Te Deum
(You Are God)

You are God: we praise you;
You are the Lord: we acclaim you;
You are the eternal Father:
All creation worships you.

To you all angels, all the powers of heaven,
Cherubim and Seraphim, sing in endless praise:
  Holy, holy, holy Lord, God of power and might,
  heaven and earth are full of your glory.

The glorious company of apostles praise you.
The noble fellowship of prophets praise you.
The white-robed army of martyrs praise you.
Throughout the world the holy Church acclaims you:
  Father, of majesty unbounded,
your true and only Son, worthy of all worship,
  and the Holy Spirit, advocate and guide.

You, Christ, are the king of glory,
the eternal Son of the Father.

When you became man to set us free
you did not spurn the Virgin's womb.

You overcame the sting of death,
and opened the kingdom of heaven to all believers.

You are seated at God's right hand in glory.
We believe that you will come, and be our judge.
  Come then, Lord, and help your people,
  bought with the price of your own blood,
  and bring us with your saints
  to glory everlasting.

Jesus, the Very Thought of Thee
St. Bernard of Clairvaux (c. 1091–1153)

Jesus! the very thought of thee
with sweetness fills my breast;
but sweeter far thy face to see,
and in thy presence rest.
No voice can sing, nor heart can frame,

nor can the memory find,
a sweeter sound than thy blest Name,
O Savior of mankind.

O Hope of every contrite heart,
O Joy of all the meek:
to those who fall, how kind thou art,
how good to those who seek.

But what to those who find? Ah, this,
no tongue nor pen can show:
the love of Jesus—what it is—
none but his loved ones know.
O Fount of Mercy! Light of Heaven!
Our darkness cast away,
and grant us all, through thee forgiven,
to see the perfect day!

Trinity Praises

Praise to the Father, with the Son,
and Holy Spirit, Three in One:
as ever was in ages past,
and shall be so while ages last. Amen.

Psalm 8

O LORD, our Sovereign,
   how majestic is your name in all the earth!
You have set your glory above the heavens.
   Out of the mouths of babes and infants
you have founded a bulwark because of your foes,
   to silence the enemy and the avenger.
When I look at your heavens, the work of your fingers,
   the moon and the stars that you have established;
what are human beings that you are mindful of them,
   mortals that you care for them?
Yet you have made them a little lower than God,
   and crowned them with glory and honor.
You have given them dominion over the works of your
      hands;
   you have put all things under their feet,
all sheep and oxen,
   and also the beasts of the field,
the birds of the air, and the fish of the sea,
   whatever passes along the paths of the seas.
O LORD, our Sovereign,
   how majestic is your name in all the earth!

Psalm 116:1-9

I love the LORD, because he has heard
    my voice and my supplications.
Because he inclined his ear to me,
    therefore I will call on him as long as I live.
The snares of death encompassed me;
    the pangs of Sheol laid hold on me;
    I suffered distress and anguish.
Then I called on the name of the LORD:
    "O LORD, I pray, save my life!"
Gracious is the LORD, and righteous;
    our God is merciful.
The LORD protects the simple;
    when I was brought low, he saved me.
Return, O my soul, to your rest,
    for the LORD has dealt bountifully with you.
For you have delivered my soul from death,
    my eyes from tears,
    my feet from stumbling.
I walk before the LORD
    in the land of the living.

Glory Be to Jesus

Glory be to Jesus, who in bitter pains
poured for me the lifeblood from his sacred veins.

Grace and life eternal in that blood I find,
blessed be his compassion infinitely kind.

Blessed through endless ages be the precious stream
which from sin and sorrow doth the world redeem.

Oft as earth, exulting, wafts its praise on high,
angel hosts, rejoicing, make their glad reply.

Lift ye then your voices; swell the mighty flood;
louder still and louder praise the precious blood. Amen.

Psalm 63:1-8

O God, you are my God, I seek you,
    my soul thirsts for you;
my flesh faints for you,
    as in a dry and weary land where there is no water.
So I have looked upon you in the sanctuary,

beholding your power and glory.
Because your steadfast love is better than life,
    my lips will praise you.
So I will bless you as long as I live;
    I will lift up my hands and call on your name.
My soul is satisfied as with a rich feast,
    and my mouth praises you with joyful lips
when I think of you on my bed,
    and meditate on you in the watches of the night;
for you have been my help,
    and in the shadow of your wings I sing for joy.
My soul clings to you;
    your right hand upholds me.

Chapter 5 | PRAYERS ON THE RUN

Take one or two of the thoughts that have most moved you in prayer, and that you think, before God, to be the most useful. These thoughts will supply you, during the day, with ejaculatory prayers.

—St. Francis de Sales (1567–1622)

Though I walk in the shadow of death, I will fear no evil, for you are with me.

(see Psalm 23:4)

O Jesus, give me courage.

(see Psalm 27:14; 31:24)

O Lord, show me your ways and teach me your paths.

(see Psalm 25:4)

Jesus, meek and humble, make my heart like yours.

—Litany of the Sacred Heart

In mercy, remember me, for your goodness' sake.

(see Psalm 25:6-7)

O Lord, help us and redeem us, for your name's sake.

(see Psalm 44:26; 79:9)

Give thanks to the Lord, for he is good; for his steadfast love endures forever.

(see Psalm 107:1, 118:1)

O Jesus, be my protector—a house of refuge to save me.

(see Psalm 31:2)

O Jesus, my creator, create in me a clean heart and renew a right spirit within me.

(see Psalm 51:10)

O Jesus, our physician, heal my soul, for I have sinned against you.

(see Psalm 41:4)

May the will of God be done in all things.

—Litany of Resignation to the Will of God

Give peace, O Lord, in our days.

—Litany to the Lamb of God in Time of War

O God, be merciful to me, a sinner.

Jesus, Son of the living God, have mercy on me.

—Litany of the Most Holy Name of Jesus

O God, come to my assistance. O Lord, hurry to help me.

(see Psalm 70:1)

Lord, show me the road I must travel for you to relieve my heart.

—Psalm 143:8 (NJB)

Lord, make sure that I am not on my way to ruin and guide me on the road to eternal life.

(see Psalm 139:24)

Good Jesus, have mercy on me.

—Prayer in Honor of
the Most Holy Name of Jesus

Grant me grace to fix my mind on you.

—The Jesus Psalter

Protect me under the shadow of your wings.

(see Psalm 17:8)

Save us, waking, that we may watch with Christ.
Save us, sleeping, that we may rest in peace.

—The Daily Office

The God of all comfort, comfort us in all our troubles.

(see 2 Corinthians 1:3-4)

O Savior of the world, save us and help us.

—Morning Prayer,
The Book of Common Prayer

Heart of Jesus, burning with love of us, inflame our
hearts with love of you.

—Prayer to the Sacred Heart

Jesus, my God, I love you above all things.

—Act of Contrition

Jesus, I trust in you.

—Divine Mercy Devotion

Mother of God, intercede for us.

—Marian Antiphon

Mary, Mother of God and mother of mercy, pray for me and for the departed.

—St. Philip Neri

O Mary, conceived without sin, pray for us who have recourse to you.

—Miraculous Medal Prayer

PART 2

PRAYER AND THE SACRAMENTS

The liturgy of the Mass is the celebration of the central mystery of redemption. It is in a way the only event we can participate in, whose reality is rooted in both eternity and time.

—Benedict Groeschel, CFR

The celebration of the Eucharist is the heart of the communal prayer of the Catholic Church. The Eucharistic Prayer, though spoken by a priest, is ours also, as we join our hearts with his and with the company of saints. The liturgy allows for very earthbound intercessions, where we ask for God's direction, intervention, comfort, and healing. We've included the four versions of the Eucharistic Prayer, which are variously used by priests, depending on the liturgical season or personal preference.

After the Eucharistic liturgy, we turn to prayers that help us prepare to receive the Sacraments of Reconciliation and the Anointing of the Sick. Most parishes offer the Sacrament of Reconciliation at regularly scheduled times. Many parishes celebrate the Anointing of the Sick during certain Sunday liturgies. You may also make an appointment with a priest to celebrate either of these sacraments.

Finally, this section wouldn't be complete without prayers of adoration to the Blessed Sacrament. We've selected a number of traditional devotional prayers that could be used by individuals or groups in church and at special times when the Blessed Sacrament is presented for adoration.

Chapter 6 | TO PRAY BEFORE, DURING, AND AFTER MASS

A Prayer Before Mass
St. Thomas Aquinas (c. 1225–c. 1275)

Almighty and ever-living God, I approach the sacrament of your only-begotten Son, our Lord Jesus Christ, I come sick to the doctor of life, unclean to the fountain of mercy, blind to the radiance of eternal light, and poor and needy to the Lord of heaven and earth. Lord, in your great generosity, heal my sickness, wash away my defilement, enlighten my blindness, enrich my poverty, and clothe my nakedness. May I receive the bread of angels, the King of kings and Lord of lords, with humble reverence, with the purity and faith, the repentance and love, and the determined purpose that will help to bring me to salvation. May I receive the sacrament of the Lord's Body and Blood, and its reality and power.

Kind God, may I receive the Body of your only-begotten Son, our Lord Jesus Christ, born from the womb of the Virgin Mary, and so be received into his mystical body and numbered among his members.

Loving father, as on my earthly pilgrimage I now receive your beloved Son under the veil of a sacrament, may I one day see him face to face in glory, who lives and reigns with you forever. Amen.

A Prayer After Mass
St. Thomas Aquinas (c. 1225–c. 1275)

I thank you, holy Lord, almighty Father, everlasting God, because you have seen fit to satisfy me, a sinner, your unworthy servant, for no merits of my own, but only by the condescension of your mercy, with the precious body and blood of your Son, our Lord Jesus Christ.

I ask that this Holy Communion may be to me, not guilt for punishment, but saving intercession for pardon.

May it be to me the armor of faith and the shield of good will.

May it be to me the evacuation of my faults, the extermination of lust, the augmentation of charity and patience, of humility and obedience; the strong defense against the snares of all my enemies, visible as well as invisible; the perfect quieting of my impulses, both carnal and spiritual; my firm adhesion to you my one and true God; and the happy consummation of my end.

And I pray that you would see fit to bring me, a sinner, to that indescribable feast, where you, with your Son and the Holy Spirit, are to your saints true light, full contentment, everlasting joy, consummate pleasure, and perfect happiness. Through the same Christ, our Lord. Amen.

Eucharistic Hymn
St. Bernard of Clairvaux (c. 1091–1153)

O Jesus, joy of loving hearts,
O Fount of life, O Light of men,
from the best bliss that earth imparts
we turn unfilled to you again.

We taste of you, O living Bread,
and long to feast upon you still;
we drink of you, the fountainhead,
and our souls' thirst find you to fill.

O Jesus, ever with us stay,
make all our moments calm and bright;
chase the dark night of sin away,
shed o'er the world your holy light.

Chapter 7 | THE PRAYERS OF THE MASS

Liturgy of the Word

Profession of Faith: Nicene Creed

I believe in one God,
the Father almighty,
maker of heaven and earth,
of all things visible and invisible.

I believe in one Lord Jesus Christ,
the Only Begotten Son of God,
born of the Father before all ages.
God from God, Light from Light,
true God from true God,
begotten, not made, consubstantial with the Father;
through him all things were made.
For us men and for our salvation
he came down from heaven,
and by the Holy Spirit was incarnate of the
    Virgin Mary,
and became man.

For our sake he was crucified under Pontius Pilate,
he suffered death and was buried,
and rose again on the third day
in accordance with the Scriptures.
He ascended into heaven
and is seated at the right hand of the Father.
He will come again in glory
to judge the living and the dead
and his kingdom will have no end.

I believe in the Holy Spirit, the Lord, the giver of life,
who proceeds from the Father and the Son,
who with the Father and the Son is adored and glorified,
who has spoken through the prophets.

I believe in one, holy, catholic and apostolic Church.
I confess one Baptism for the forgiveness of sins
and I look forward to the resurrection of the dead
and the life of the world to come. Amen.

Liturgy of the Eucharist

Eucharistic Prayer I

Preface
(as chosen in accord with the rubrics)

Preface Acclamation

Holy, Holy, Holy Lord God of hosts.
Heaven and earth are full of your glory.
Hosanna in the highest.
Blessed is he who comes in the name of the Lord.
Hosanna in the highest.

To you, therefore, most merciful Father,
we make humble prayer and petition
through Jesus Christ, your Son, our Lord:
that you accept
and bless these gifts, these offerings,
these holy and unblemished sacrifices,
which we offer you firstly
for your holy catholic Church.
Be pleased to grant her peace,

to guard, unite and govern her
throughout the whole world,
together with your servant N. our Pope
and N. our Bishop,
and all those who, holding to the truth,
hand on the catholic and apostolic faith.

Remember, Lord, your servants N. and N.
and all gathered here,
whose faith and devotion are known to you.
For them, we offer you this sacrifice of praise
or they offer it for themselves
and all who are dear to them:
for the redemption of their souls,
in hope of health and well-being,
and paying their homage to you,
the eternal God, living and true.

In communion with those whose memory we venerate,
especially the glorious ever-Virgin Mary,
Mother of our God and Lord, Jesus Christ,
and blessed Joseph, her Spouse,
your blessed Apostles and Martyrs,
Peter and Paul, Andrew,

(James, John,
Thomas, James, Philip,
Bartholomew, Matthew,
Simon and Jude;
Linus, Cletus, Clement, Sixtus,
Cornelius, Cyprian,
Lawrence, Chrysogonus,
John and Paul,
Cosmas and Damian)
and all your Saints;
we ask that through their merits and prayers,
in all things we may be defended
by your protecting help.
(Through Christ our Lord. Amen.)

Therefore, Lord, we pray:
graciously accept this oblation of our service,
that of your whole family;
order our days in your peace,
and command that we be delivered from eternal
    damnation
and counted among the flock of those you have chosen.
(Through Christ our Lord. Amen.)

Be pleased, O God, we pray,
to bless, acknowledge,
and approve this offering in every respect;
make it spiritual and acceptable,
so that it may become for us
the Body and Blood of your most beloved Son,
our Lord Jesus Christ.

On the day before he was to suffer,
he took bread in his holy and venerable hands,
and with eyes raised to heaven
to you, O God, his almighty Father,
giving you thanks, he said the blessing,
broke the bread
and gave it to his disciples, saying:

TAKE THIS, ALL OF YOU, AND EAT OF IT,
FOR THIS IS MY BODY,
WHICH WILL BE GIVEN UP FOR YOU.

In a similar way, when supper was ended,
he took this precious chalice
in his holy and venerable hands,

and once more giving you thanks, he said the blessing
and gave the chalice to his disciples, saying:

TAKE THIS, ALL OF YOU, AND DRINK FROM IT,
FOR THIS IS THE CHALICE OF MY BLOOD,
THE BLOOD OF THE NEW AND ETERNAL COVENANT,
WHICH WILL BE POURED OUT FOR YOU AND FOR MANY
FOR THE FORGIVENESS OF SINS.

DO THIS IN MEMORY OF ME.

Memorial Acclamation

The mystery of faith.

We proclaim your Death, O Lord,
and profess your Resurrection
until you come again.

　　Or:

When we eat this Bread and drink this Cup,
we proclaim your Death, O Lord,
until you come again.

　　Or:

Save us, Savior of the world,

for by your Cross and Resurrection
you have set us free.

Therefore, O Lord,
as we celebrate the memorial of the blessed Passion,
the Resurrection from the dead,
and the glorious Ascension into heaven
of Christ, your Son, our Lord,
we, your servants and your holy people,
offer to your glorious majesty
from the gifts that you have given us,
this pure victim,
this holy victim,
this spotless victim,
the holy Bread of eternal life
and the Chalice of everlasting salvation.

Be pleased to look upon these offerings
with a serene and kindly countenance,
and to accept them,
as once you were pleased to accept
the gifts of your servant Abel the just,
the sacrifice of Abraham, our father in faith,

and the offering of your high priest Melchizedek,
a holy sacrifice, a spotless victim.

In humble prayer we ask you, almighty God:
command that these gifts be borne
by the hands of your holy Angel
to your altar on high
in the sight of your divine majesty,
so that all of us, who through this participation
    at the altar
receive the most holy Body and Blood of your Son,
may be filled with every grace and heavenly blessing.
(Through Christ our Lord. Amen.)

Remember also, Lord, your servants N. and N.,
who have gone before us with the sign of faith
and rest in the sleep of peace.
Grant them, O Lord, we pray,
and all who sleep in Christ,
a place of refreshment, light and peace.
(Through Christ our Lord. Amen.)

To us, also, your servants, who, though sinners,
hope in your abundant mercies,

graciously grant some share
and fellowship with your holy Apostles and Martyrs:
with John the Baptist, Stephen,
Matthias, Barnabas,
(Ignatius, Alexander,
Marcellinus, Peter,
Felicity, Perpetua,
Agatha, Lucy,
Agnes, Cecilia, Anastasia)
and all your Saints;
admit us, we beseech you,
into their company,
not weighing our merits,
but granting us your pardon,
through Christ our Lord.

Through whom
you continue to make all these good things, O Lord;
you sanctify them, fill them with life,
bless them, and bestow them upon us.

Concluding Doxology

Through him, and with him, and in him,

O God, almighty Father,
in the unity of the Holy Spirit,
all glory and honor is yours,
for ever and ever.
Amen.

Eucharistic Prayer II

Although it is provided with its own Preface, Eucharistic
Prayer II *may also be used with other* Prefaces,
*especially those that present an overall view of the
mystery of salvation, such as the* Common Prefaces.

Preface

It is truly right and just, our duty and our salvation,
always and everywhere to give you thanks, Father
    most holy,
through your beloved Son, Jesus Christ,
your Word through whom you made all things,
whom you sent as our Savior and Redeemer,
incarnate by the Holy Spirit and born of the Virgin.

Fulfilling your will and gaining for you a holy people,
he stretched out his hands as he endured his Passion,

so as to break the bonds of death and manifest
the resurrection.

And so, with the Angels and all the Saints
we declare your glory,
as with one voice we acclaim:

Preface Acclamation

Holy, Holy, Holy Lord God of hosts.
Heaven and earth are full of your glory.
Hosanna in the highest.
Blessed is he who comes in the name of the Lord.
Hosanna in the highest.

You are indeed Holy, O Lord,
the fount of all holiness.
Make holy, therefore, these gifts, we pray,
by sending down your Spirit upon them like the dewfall,
so that they may become for us
the Body and Blood of our Lord Jesus Christ.

At the time he was betrayed
and entered willingly into his Passion,

he took bread and, giving thanks, broke it,
and gave it to his disciples, saying:

TAKE THIS, ALL OF YOU, AND EAT OF IT,
FOR THIS IS MY BODY,
WHICH WILL BE GIVEN UP FOR YOU.

In a similar way, when supper was ended,
he took the chalice
and, once more giving thanks,
he gave it to his disciples, saying:

TAKE THIS, ALL OF YOU, AND DRINK FROM IT,
FOR THIS IS THE CHALICE OF MY BLOOD,
THE BLOOD OF THE NEW AND ETERNAL COVENANT,
WHICH WILL BE POURED OUT FOR YOU AND FOR MANY
FOR THE FORGIVENESS OF SINS.

DO THIS IN MEMORY OF ME.

Memorial Acclamation

The mystery of faith.

We proclaim your Death, O Lord,

and profess your Resurrection
until you come again.

Or:

When we eat this Bread and drink this Cup,
we proclaim your Death, O Lord,
until you come again.

Or:

Save us, Savior of the world,
for by your Cross and Resurrection
you have set us free.

Therefore, as we celebrate
the memorial of his Death and Resurrection,
we offer you, Lord,
the Bread of life and the Chalice of salvation,
giving thanks that you have held us worthy
to be in your presence and minister to you.

Humbly we pray
that, partaking of the Body and Blood of Christ,
we may be gathered into one by the Holy Spirit.

Remember, Lord, your Church,
spread throughout the world,

and bring her to the fullness of charity,
together with N. our Pope and N. our Bishop
and all the clergy.

Remember also our brothers and sisters
who have fallen asleep in the hope of the resurrection,
and all who have died in your mercy:
welcome them into the light of your face.
Have mercy on us all, we pray,
that with the Blessed Virgin Mary, Mother of God,
with the blessed Apostles,
and all the Saints who have pleased you throughout
   the ages,
we may merit to be coheirs to eternal life,
and may praise and glorify you
through your Son, Jesus Christ.

Concluding Doxology

Through him, and with him, and in him,
O God, almighty Father,
in the unity of the Holy Spirit,

all glory and honor is yours,
for ever and ever.
Amen.

Eucharistic Prayer III

Preface
(as chosen in accord with the rubrics)

Preface Acclamation

Holy, Holy, Holy Lord God of hosts.
Heaven and earth are full of your glory.
Hosanna in the highest.
Blessed is he who comes in the name of the Lord.
Hosanna in the highest.

You are indeed Holy, O Lord,
and all you have created
rightly gives you praise,
for through your Son our Lord Jesus Christ,
by the power and working of the Holy Spirit,
you give life to all things and make them holy,
and you never cease to gather a people to yourself,

so that from the rising of the sun to its setting
a pure sacrifice may be offered to your name.

Therefore, O Lord, we humbly implore you:
by the same Spirit graciously make holy
these gifts we have brought to you for consecration,
that they may become the Body and Blood
of your Son our Lord Jesus Christ,
at whose command we celebrate these mysteries.

For on the night he was betrayed
he himself took bread,
and, giving you thanks, he said the blessing,
broke the bread and gave it to his disciples, saying:

TAKE THIS, ALL OF YOU, AND EAT OF IT,
FOR THIS IS MY BODY,
WHICH WILL BE GIVEN UP FOR YOU.

In a similar way, when supper was ended,
he took the chalice,
and, giving you thanks, he said the blessing,
and gave the chalice to his disciples, saying:

TAKE THIS, ALL OF YOU, AND DRINK FROM IT,
FOR THIS IS THE CHALICE OF MY BLOOD,
THE BLOOD OF THE NEW AND ETERNAL COVENANT,
WHICH WILL BE POURED OUT FOR YOU AND FOR MANY
FOR THE FORGIVENESS OF SINS.

DO THIS IN MEMORY OF ME.

Memorial Acclamation

The mystery of faith.

We proclaim your Death, O Lord,
and profess your Resurrection
until you come again.
   Or:
When we eat this Bread and drink this Cup,
we proclaim your Death, O Lord,
until you come again.
   Or:
Save us, Savior of the world,
for by your Cross and Resurrection
you have set us free.

Therefore, O Lord, as we celebrate the memorial
of the saving Passion of your Son,
his wondrous Resurrection
and Ascension into heaven,
and as we look forward to his second coming,
we offer you in thanksgiving
this holy and living sacrifice.

Look, we pray, upon the oblation of your Church
and, recognizing the sacrificial Victim by whose death
you willed to reconcile us to yourself,
grant that we, who are nourished
by the Body and Blood of your Son
and filled with his Holy Spirit,
may become one body, one spirit in Christ.

May he make of us
an eternal offering to you,
so that we may obtain an inheritance with your elect,
especially with the most Blessed Virgin Mary, Mother
    of God,
with your blessed Apostles and glorious Martyrs
(with Saint N.: *the Saint of the day or Patron Saint*)
and with all the Saints,

on whose constant intercession in your presence
we rely for unfailing help.

May this Sacrifice of our reconciliation,
we pray, O Lord,
advance the peace and salvation of all the world.
Be pleased to confirm in faith and charity
your pilgrim Church on earth,
with your servant N. our Pope and N. our Bishop,
the Order of Bishops, all the clergy,
and the entire people you have gained for your own.

Listen graciously to the prayers of this family,
whom you have summoned before you:
in your compassion, O merciful Father,
gather to yourself all your children
scattered throughout the world.
To our departed brothers and sisters
and to all who were pleasing to you
at their passing from this life,
give kind admittance to your kingdom.
There we hope to enjoy for ever the fullness of
    your glory
through Christ our Lord,

through whom you bestow on the world all that
   is good.

Concluding Doxology

Through him, and with him, and in him,
O God, almighty Father,
in the unity of the Holy Spirit,
all glory and honor is yours,
for ever and ever.
Amen.

Eucharistic Prayer IV

Only the following Preface *may be said with* Eucharistic
Prayer IV *because of the structure of the* Prayer *itself,
which presents a summary of salvation history.*

Preface

It is truly right to give you thanks,
truly just to give you glory, Father most holy,
for you are the one God living and true,
existing before all ages and abiding for all eternity,

dwelling in unapproachable light;
yet you, who alone are good, the source of life,
have made all that is,
so that you might fill your creatures with blessings
and bring joy to many of them by the glory of
   your light.

And so, in your presence are countless hosts of Angels,
who serve you day and night
and, gazing upon the glory of your face,
glorify you without ceasing.

With them we, too, confess your name in exultation,
giving voice to every creature under heaven,
as we acclaim:

Preface Acclamation

Holy, Holy, Holy Lord God of hosts.
Heaven and earth are full of your glory.
Hosanna in the highest.
Blessed is he who comes in the name of the Lord.
Hosanna in the highest.

We give you praise, Father most holy,
for you are great
and you have fashioned all your works
in wisdom and in love.
You formed man in your own image
and entrusted the whole world to his care,
so that in serving you alone, the Creator,
he might have dominion over all creatures.
And when through disobedience he had lost your
    friendship,
you did not abandon him to the domain of death.
For you came in mercy to the aid of all,
so that those who seek might find you.
Time and again you offered them covenants
and through the prophets
taught them to look forward to salvation.

And you so loved the world, Father most holy,
that in the fullness of time
you sent your Only Begotten Son to be our Savior.
Made incarnate by the Holy Spirit
and born of the Virgin Mary,
he shared our human nature
in all things but sin.

To the poor he proclaimed the good news of salvation,
to prisoners, freedom,
and to the sorrowful of heart, joy.
To accomplish your plan,
he gave himself up to death,
and, rising from the dead,
he destroyed death and restored life.

And that we might live no longer for ourselves
but for him who died and rose again for us,
he sent the Holy Spirit from you, Father,
as the first fruits for those who believe,
so that, bringing to perfection his work in the world,
he might sanctify creation to the full.

Therefore, O Lord, we pray:
may this same Holy Spirit
graciously sanctify these offerings,
that they may become
the Body and Blood of our Lord Jesus Christ
for the celebration of this great mystery,
which he himself left us
as an eternal covenant.

For when the hour had come
for him to be glorified by you, Father most holy,
having loved his own who were in the world,
he loved them to the end:
and while they were at supper,
he took bread, blessed and broke it,
and gave it to his disciples, saying:

TAKE THIS, ALL OF YOU, AND EAT OF IT,
FOR THIS IS MY BODY,
WHICH WILL BE GIVEN UP FOR YOU.

In a similar way,
taking the chalice filled with the fruit of the vine,
he gave thanks,
and gave the chalice to his disciples, saying:

TAKE THIS, ALL OF YOU, AND DRINK FROM IT,
FOR THIS IS THE CHALICE OF MY BLOOD,
THE BLOOD OF THE NEW AND ETERNAL COVENANT,
WHICH WILL BE POURED OUT FOR YOU AND FOR MANY
FOR THE FORGIVENESS OF SINS.

DO THIS IN MEMORY OF ME.

Memorial Acclamation

The mystery of faith.

We proclaim your Death, O Lord,
and profess your Resurrection
until you come again.
   Or:
When we eat this Bread and drink this Cup,
we proclaim your Death, O Lord,
until you come again.
   Or:
Save us, Savior of the world,
for by your Cross and Resurrection
you have set us free.

Therefore, O Lord,
as we now celebrate the memorial of our redemption,
we remember Christ's Death
and his descent to the realm of the dead,
we proclaim his Resurrection
and his Ascension to your right hand,
and, as we await his coming in glory,
we offer you his Body and Blood,

the sacrifice acceptable to you
which brings salvation to the whole world.

Look, O Lord, upon the Sacrifice
which you yourself have provided for your Church,
and grant in your loving kindness
to all who partake of this one Bread and one Chalice
that, gathered into one body by the Holy Spirit,
they may truly become a living sacrifice in Christ
to the praise of your glory.

Therefore, Lord, remember now
all for whom we offer this sacrifice:
especially your servant N. our Pope,
N. our Bishop, and the whole Order of Bishops,
all the clergy,
those who take part in this offering,
those gathered here before you,
your entire people,
and all who seek you with a sincere heart.

Remember also
those who have died in the peace of your Christ

and all the dead,
whose faith you alone have known.

To all of us, your children,
grant, O merciful Father,
that we may enter into a heavenly inheritance
with the Blessed Virgin Mary, Mother of God,
and with your Apostles and Saints in your kingdom.
There, with the whole of creation,
freed from the corruption of sin and death,
may we glorify you through Christ our Lord,
through whom you bestow on the world all that
    is good.

Concluding Doxology

Through him, and with him, and in him,
O God, almighty Father,
in the unity of the Holy Spirit,
all glory and honor is yours,
for ever and ever.
Amen.

Chapter 8 | PREPARING FOR THE SACRAMENT OF RECONCILIATION

A Prayer Before Confession

O Lord God, enlighten my heart with the brightness of your grace, that I may truly know my failings and sins and confess them with sorrow and contrition, as it is right to do in the presence of you and your minister, the priest, and of Mary, and of all the saints, that I may make full satisfaction for my sins and amend them to your praise and glory and to the salvation of my soul. Amen.

Isaiah 55:6-11

Seek the LORD while he may be found,
    call upon him while he is near;
let the wicked forsake their way,
    and the unrighteous their thoughts;
let them return to the LORD,
that he may have mercy on them,
    and to our God, for he will abundantly pardon.
For my thoughts are not your thoughts,
    nor are your ways my ways, says the LORD.

For as the heavens are higher than the earth,
    so are my ways higher than your ways
    and my thoughts than your thoughts.
For as the rain and the snow come down from heaven,
    and do not return there until they have watered
      the earth,
making it bring forth and sprout,
    giving seed to the sower and bread to the eater,
so shall my word be that goes out from my mouth;
    it shall not return to me empty,
but it shall accomplish that which I purpose,
    and succeed in the thing for which I sent it.

Wisdom 11:21–12:2, NJB

For your great power is always at your service,
and who can withstand the might of your arm?
The whole world, for you, can no more than tip
    a balance,
like a drop of morning dew falling on the ground.
Yet you are merciful to all, because you are almighty,
you overlook people's sins, so that they can repent.
Yes, you love everything that exists,
and nothing that you have made disgusts you,

since, if you had hated something, you would not have
    made it.
And how could a thing subsist, had you not willed it?
Or how be preserved, if not called forth by you?
No, you spare all, since all is yours, Lord, lover of life!
For your imperishable spirit is in everything!
And thus, gradually, you correct those who offend;
you admonish and remind them of how they have sinned,
so that they may abstain from evil and trust in you, Lord.

Psalm 51:1-4, 10-12

Have mercy on me, O God,
    according to your steadfast love;
according to your abundant mercy
    blot out my transgressions.
Wash me thoroughly from my iniquity,
    and cleanse me from my sin.
For I know my transgressions,
    and my sin is ever before me.
Against you, you alone, have I sinned,
    and done what is evil in your sight,
so that you are justified in your sentence
    and blameless when you pass judgment. . . .

Create in me a clean heart, O God,
  and put a new and right spirit within me.
Do not cast me away from your presence,
  and do not take your holy spirit from me.
Restore to me the joy of your salvation
  and sustain in me a willing spirit.

An Examination of Conscience

1 Peter 2:24 says that Jesus "bore our sins in his body on the cross, so that, free from sin, we might live for righteousness." Let's enter more fully into the freedom that God has for us by turning to him in repentance. In the Sacrament of Reconciliation we can experience Jesus not only forgiving us, but also transforming and strengthening us.

The following examination of conscience is meant to help you prepare for confession. As you ponder the verses, ask the Holy Spirit to show you any hidden corners of your life that need to be transformed.

- Does God hold first place in my life, or have I allowed myself to become the servant of money, popularity, success, or anything else?

- Have I given priority to God on Sundays and holy days by attending Mass and making a special effort to seek him?

- Have I nourished my love and knowledge of God through regular prayer and Scripture reading?

- Are there areas of myself that I am holding back from God? What secret parts of my life do I not want to expose to God's light and love?

- How am I doing in my relationships with the people God is calling me to love and serve: family members, friends, co-workers, neighbors, parishioners? Am I treating them with dignity and respect?

- Do I give appropriate honor and respect to parents, teachers, employers, and all legitimate authority?

- Is there anyone I need to forgive? Is there anyone whose forgiveness I need to ask?

- Have I been a good steward of the material things God has given me? Do I use them for his glory?

- Am I stingy with my time and gifts? Am I an active supporter and contributor to the work of the church and of organizations that serve the needy?

- Do I show compassion and concern for people who are poor, underprivileged, sick, and suffering?

- Am I vigilant about what I allow into my mind? Have I indulged in pornography, lustful thoughts, or indecent movies or conversations?

- Have I engaged in sexual activity outside marriage?

- Have I opened myself to the occult by using activities like fortune telling, palm reading, and astrology?

- Have I used my gift of speech to build up and not to tear down? Have I lied or gossiped about other people in a way that damaged their reputations?

- Do my words reveal a love for the Lord? Have I misused his name? Have I held back from speaking the truth or expressing my faith when I should have?

- Have my words led anyone into sin? What about my nonverbal communication?

Prayers After Confession

Act of Contrition
Traditional Version

O my God,
I am heartily sorry for
having offended you,
and I detest all my sins,
because I dread the loss of heaven,
and the pains of hell;
but most of all because
they offend you, my God,
who are all good and
deserving of all my love.
I firmly resolve,
with the help of your grace,
to confess my sins,
to do penance,
and to amend my life. Amen.

Act of Contrition
Contemporary Version

My God,
I am sorry for my sins
with all my heart.
In choosing to do wrong
and failing to do good,
I have sinned against you,
whom I should love above all things.
I firmly intend,
with your help,
to do penance,
to sin no more,
and to avoid whatever leads me to sin.
Our Savior Jesus Christ
suffered and died for us;
in his name, my God, have mercy. Amen.

Confiteor

I confess to almighty God
and to you, my brothers and sisters,
that I have greatly sinned,

in my thoughts and in my words,
in what I have done and in what I have failed to do,
through my fault, through my fault,
through my most grievous fault;
therefore I ask blessed Mary ever-Virgin,
all the Angels and Saints,
and you, my brothers and sisters,
to pray for me to the Lord our God.

May almighty God have mercy on us,
forgive us our sins,
and bring us to everlasting life.
Amen.

Prayer Before a Crucifix

Look down upon me, good and gentle Jesus, while before your face I humbly kneel and ask you to fix deep in my heart lively faith, hope, and charity; true contrition for my sins; and firm purpose of amendment; while I contemplate with great love and tender grief your five wounds; while I call to mind the words your prophet David said of you, my Jesus: "They pierced my hands and my feet; they numbered all my bones" (see Psalm 22:17).

Chapter 9 | PREPARING FOR THE SACRAMENT OF ANOINTING OF THE SICK

Hear Us on Behalf of the Sick

Almighty, everlasting God, the eternal salvation of those who believe: hear us on behalf of your servants who are sick, for whom we humbly crave the help of your mercy, that, being restored to health, they may give thanks to you in your church, through our Lord, Jesus Christ. Amen.

Reflection on James 5:13-16

Are any among you suffering? They should pray. Are any cheerful? They should sing songs of praise. Are any among you sick? They should call for the elders of the church and have them pray over them, anointing them with oil in the name of the Lord. The prayer of faith will save the sick, and the Lord will raise them up; and anyone who has committed sins will be forgiven. Therefore confess your sins to one another, and pray for one another, so that you may be healed. The prayer of the righteous is powerful and effective.

Mark 6:7, 12-13

He called the twelve and began to send them out two by two, and gave them authority over the unclean spirits. . . . So they went out and proclaimed that all should repent. They cast out many demons, and anointed with oil many who were sick and cured them.

Psalm 130:1-6

Out of the depths I cry to you, O LORD.
    Lord, hear my voice!
Let your ears be attentive
    to the voice of my supplications!

If you, O LORD, should mark iniquities,
    Lord, who could stand?
But there is forgiveness with you,
    so that you may be revered.

I wait for the LORD, my soul waits,
    and in his word I hope;
my soul waits for the Lord

more than those who watch for the morning,
more than those who watch for the morning.

Psalm 103:1-13

Bless the LORD, O my soul,
    and all that is within me,
    bless his holy name.
Bless the LORD, O my soul,
    and do not forget all his benefits—
who forgives all your iniquity,
    who heals all your diseases,
who redeems your life from the Pit,
    who crowns you with steadfast love and mercy,
who satisfies you with good as long as you live
    so that your youth is renewed like the eagle's.
The LORD works vindication
    and justice for all who are oppressed.
He made known his ways to Moses,
    his acts to the people of Israel.
The LORD is merciful and gracious,
    slow to anger and abounding in steadfast love.
He will not always accuse,
    nor will he keep his anger forever.

He does not deal with us according to our sins,
    nor repay us according to our iniquities.
For as the heavens are high above the earth,
    so great is his steadfast love toward those who
        fear him;
as far as the east is from the west,
    so far he removes our transgressions from us.
As a father has compassion for his children,
    so the LORD has compassion for those who fear him.

Chapter 10 | ADORATION OF THE BLESSED SACRAMENT

O Saving Victim
(O Salutaris Hostia)
St. Thomas Aquinas (c. 1225–c. 1275)

O saving victim, pledge of love
who opens heaven's gate above;
by hostile wars we are oppressed,
be now our force, support, and rest.

To God the Father, and the Son,
and Holy Spirit, three in one,
be endless praise; may he above,
with life immortal, crown our love. Amen.

Anima Christi

Soul of Christ, sanctify me.
Body of Christ, heal me.
Blood of Christ, drench me.
Water from the side of Christ, wash me.

Passion of Christ, strengthen me.
Good Jesus, hear me.
In your wounds shelter me.
From turning away keep me.
From the evil one protect me.
At the hour of my death call me,
Into your presence lead me,
to praise you with all your saints
for ever and ever. Amen.

I Devoutly Adore
(Adoro te Devote)
St. Thomas Aquinas (c. 1225–c. 1275)

O Godhead hid, devoutly I adore thee,
who truly are within the forms before me:
to you my heart I bow with bended knee,
as failing quite in contemplating thee.

Sight, touch, and taste in you are each deceived;
the ear alone most safely is believed:
I believe all the Son of God has spoken,
than Truth's own word there is no truer token.

God only on the cross lay hid from view;
but here lies hid at once the manhood too:
and I, in both professing my belief,
make the same prayer as the repentant thief.

Your wounds, as Thomas saw, I do not see;
yet confess you my Lord and God to be:
make me believe you ever more and more;
in you my hope, in you my love to store.

O memorial of our Lord's own dying!
O living Bread, to mortals life supplying,
make my soul henceforth on thee to live;
ever a taste of heavenly sweetness give.

O loving Pelican! O Jesus, Lord!
unclean I am, but cleanse me in your blood:
of which a single drop, for sinners spilt,
can purge the entire world from all its guilt.

Jesus! whom for the present veiled I see,
what I so thirst for, oh, vouchsafe to me:
that I may see your countenance unfolding,
and may be blessed your glory in beholding. Amen.

Sing, My Tongue
(Pange Lingua)
St. Thomas Aquinas (c. 1225–c. 1275)

Sing, my tongue, the Savior's glory,
of his flesh the mystery sing;
of the blood, all price exceeding,
shed by our immortal King,
destined, for the world's redemption,
from a noble womb to spring.

Of a pure and spotless virgin
born for us on earth below,
he, as man with man conversing,
stayed, the seeds of truth to sow.
Then he closed in solemn order
wondrously his life of woe.

On the night of that last supper,
seated with his chosen band,
he, the paschal victim eating,
first fulfills the law's command.
Then as food to all his brethren
gives himself with his own hand.

Word made flesh, the bread of nature
by his word to flesh he turns;
wine into his blood he changes:
even though sense no change discerns.
If only the heart be in earnest,
faith her lesson quickly learns.

Down in adoration falling,
lo! the sacred host we hail;
lo! o'er ancient forms departing,
newer rites of grace prevail:
faith for all defects supplying,
where the feeble senses fail.

To the everlasting Father,
and the Son who reigns on high,
with the Holy Spirit going
forth from each eternally,
be salvation, honor, blessing,
might and endless majesty.

You gave them bread from heaven.
and therein was sweetness of every kind.

Let us pray: God, who beneath this marvelous sacrament has left us a memorial of your passion, grant us, we pray, so to venerate the sacred mysteries of your body and blood, that we may ever feel within us the fruit of your redemption, who lives and reigns forever and ever. Amen.

The Word from Above
(Verbum Supernum)
St. Thomas Aquinas (c. 1225–c. 1275)

The Word descending from above,
though with the Father still on high,
went forth upon his work of love,
and soon to life's last eve drew nigh.

He shortly to a death accursed
by a disciple shall be given;
but, to his twelve disciples, first
he gives himself, the bread from heaven.

Himself in either kind he gave;
he gave his flesh; he gave his blood;
of flesh and blood all men are made;
and he of man would be the food.

At birth, our brother he became;
at board, himself as food he gives;
to ransom us he died in shame;
as, our reward, in bliss he lives. Amen.

O saving Victim! opening wide
the gate of heaven to man below!
our foes press on from every side—
your aid supply, your strength bestow.

To your great name be endless praise,
Immortal Godhead, One in Three!
oh, grant us endless length of days,
in our true native land, with thee.

Sacred Solemnities
(Sacris Solemniis)
St. Thomas Aquinas (c. 1225–c. 1275)

Let us with hearts renewed,
our grateful homage pay,
and welcome with triumphant songs
this ever-blessed day.

Upon this hallowed night
Christ with his brethren ate
obedient to the ancient law,
the Pasch before him set.

Which done himself entire,
the true incarnate God,
alike on each, alike on all,
his sacred hands bestowed.

He gave his flesh; he gave
his precious blood; and said,
"Receive and drink ye all of this,
for your salvation shed."

Thus did the Lord appoint
this sacrifice sublime,
and made his priests its ministers
through all the bounds of time.

Farwell to types! henceforth
we feed on angels' food:
the guilty slave—oh, wonder—eats
the body of his God.

O Blessed Three in One,
visit our hearts, we pray;
and lead us on through thy own paths
to thy eternal day. Amen.

Bread of Angels
(Panis Angelicus)
St. Thomas Aquinas (c. 1225–c. 1275)

The bread of angels, bread of men is made;
the truth and substance now exclude the shade.
Oh! strange effect of love, the sovereign God
becomes the poor, the slave, the sinner's food.

O Three and One, we humbly implore
you to reveal yourself as we adore;
by your own ways, instruct us how to move
to that bright light, in which you dwell above. Amen.

Prayer for Divine Help

O my Jesus, since it is your will that the fire of your
divine love should be kindled in all hearts, fill mine with

this divine fire—with those holy flames that burn in your own most loving heart. Oh, make me sensible to your sacred presence.

My Jesus, you can do all things. Change, or destroy, in my heart everything that displeases you. Remain with me, for without you I cannot live. And grant that I may never be satisfied with anything less than you. Let me love you from this moment without ambivalence or imperfection. Cut away, destroy, absolutely and forever everything that is contrary in my soul to the purity of your love. Amen.

Divine Praises

Blessed be God.
Blessed be his holy name.
Blessed be Jesus Christ, true God and true man.
Blessed be the name of Jesus.
Blessed be the most Sacred Heart.
Blessed be his most precious blood.
Blessed be Jesus in the most holy Sacrament of the altar.
Blessed be the Holy Spirit, the Paraclete.
Blessed be the great mother of God, Mary most holy.
Blessed be her holy and Immaculate Conception.
Blessed be her glorious Assumption.

Blessed be the name of Mary, virgin and mother.
Blessed be Saint Joseph, her most chaste spouse.
Blessed be God in his angels and in his saints. Amen.

PART 3

PRAYERS TO MARY AND THE SAINTS

Let all the children of the Catholic Church . . .
continue to cherish, invoke, and beseech the Blessed
Virgin Mary, Mother of God, conceived without original
sin, and let them with entire confidence have recourse to
this sweetest Mother of grace and mercy in all dangers,
difficulties, necessities, doubts, and fears.

—Blessed Pope Pius IX

Catholic prayer is highly enriched by its awareness of the company of heaven—the saints of previous generations who have died and found their eternal reward and also the angelic hosts to whose care we are entrusted.

Of course Mary, queen of heaven, is chief among the saints, full of grace, worthy and willing to give birth to our Lord, who in turn gave his mother to the church (see John 19:27). As we intercede through Mary, she pleads our case with her son.

In this section we also include some traditional prayers to other saints, including the classic Litany of the Saints. Prayed privately or corporately, this litany pleads for the intercessions of the holy men and women whom we look to as models in their holiness and dedication to their Lord.

Chapter 11 | PRAYERS TO MARY

The Magnificat
(Canticle of Mary)

My soul proclaims the greatness of the Lord,
my spirit rejoices in God my Savior;
for he has looked with favor on his lowly servant.

From this day all generations will call me blessed;
the Almighty has done great things for me,
and holy is his Name.

He has mercy on those who fear him
in every generation.

He has shown the strength of his arm,
he has scattered the proud in their conceit.

He has cast down the mighty from their thrones,
and has lifted up the lowly.

He has filled the hungry with good things,
and the rich he has sent away empty.

He has come to the help of his servant Israel
for he has remembered the promise of his mercy,
the promise he made to our fathers,
to Abraham and his children for ever.

The Memorare
St. Bernard of Clairvaux (c. 1091–1153)

Remember, O most gracious Virgin Mary, that never
was it known that anyone who fled to your protection,
implored your help, or sought your intercession was left
unaided.

Inspired by this confidence, I fly unto you, O Virgin of
virgins, my mother; to you do I come, before you I stand,
sinful and sorrowful. O Mother of the Word Incarnate,
despise not my petitions, but in your mercy hear and
answer me. Amen.

The Angelus

The angel of the Lord declared unto Mary:
and she conceived by the Holy Spirit.
    Hail Mary . . .
Behold the handmaid of the Lord:

be it done unto me according to your word.

    Hail Mary . . .

And the Word was made flesh:

and dwelt among us.

    Hail Mary . . .

Pray for us, holy mother of God:

that we may be made worthy of the promises of Christ.

Pour down your grace into our souls, we beseech you, O Lord, that we, unto whom the incarnation of Christ your Son was made known by the message of an angel, may, by his passion and cross, be brought to the glory of the resurrection. Through the same Christ our Lord. Amen.

Queen of Heaven
(Regina Coeli)

Queen of Heaven, rejoice. Alleluia.

For he whom you were made worthy to bear. Alleluia.

Has risen as he said. Alleluia.

Pray for us to our God. Alleluia.

Rejoice and be glad, O Virgin Mary. Alleluia.

For the Lord has risen indeed. Alleluia.

God, who through the resurrection of your Son, our Lord Jesus Christ, has made glad the whole world, grant us, we pray, that through the intercession of the virgin Mary, his mother, we may attain the joys of eternal life. Through the same Christ our Lord. Amen.

Hail, August Queen of Peace

Hail, august Queen of Peace! Hail, holiest Mother of God! By the sacred heart of Jesus, your son, the prince of peace, grant that his anger may end, and that in peace he may reign over us. Remember, O most loving Virgin Mary, that no one ever sought your mediation without obtaining relief. Animated with this confidence, I come to you. Do not, O Mother of the Word, despise my words; but hear and grant my prayer, O merciful, O sweet Virgin Mary. Amen.

Prayer to Our Lady of Guadalupe

Our Lady of Guadalupe, mystical rose, intercede for the church, protect the Holy Father, help all who invoke you in their necessities. Since you are the ever Virgin Mary and Mother of the true God, obtain for us from your most holy son the grace of a firm faith and sure hope amid the bitterness of life, as well as an ardent love and the precious gift of final perseverance. Amen.

Virgin, Faithful Pure
St. Louis de Montfort (1673–1716)

Virgin, faithful pure, God's chosen mother,
fill me with a measure of your faith;
that way will Wisdom come to me
and all his attendant treasures.

I Choose You for My Mother
St. Francis de Sales (1567–1622)

I salute you, most loving Virgin Mary, mother of God, and choose you for my most dear mother. I beg you to accept me as your child and servant. I desire no other mother or mistress but you. I entreat you, my good, kind and sweet Mother, to remember that I am your child, that you are most powerful, and that I am a poor, sinful, and weak creature. I beg you also, to direct and support me in all my undertakings, for I am poor and need your gracious assistance and protection.

Most holy Virgin, my sweet Mother, let me participate in all your virtues, particularly in your holy humility, your perfect purity, and your fervent charity, but above all grant me [name your petition]. . . .

Let your name be exalted and by your intercession obtain for me all favors and graces of the holy Trinity, Father, Son, and Holy Spirit, the object of all my love for time and eternity. Amen.

I Commend and Commit
St. Aloysius Gonzaga (1568–1591)

Most holy Mary, my Lady, to your faithful care and special keeping and to the bosom of your mercy, today and every day, and particularly at the hour of my death, I commend my soul and my body; all my hope and consolation, all my trials and miseries, my life and the end of my life I commit to you, that through your most holy intercession and by your merits all my actions may be directed and ordered according to your will and that of your divine Son. Amen.

Prayer to Mary for a Good Death

O Mary, conceived without sin, pray for us who have recourse to you. O Refuge of Sinners, do not abandon us in the hour of our death, but obtain for us perfect sorrow, sincere contrition, remission of our sins, a worthy reception of the most Holy Communion, the strengthening effect of the sacrament of anointing, that we may present ourselves with security before the throne of the just, but likewise merciful, judge, our God and Redeemer. Amen.

From the Stabat Mater

The Stabat Mater *is an ancient hymn about Mary's sorrow at Jesus' crucifixion. Part of the hymn is a prayer:*

Holy Mother, fount of love,
touch my spirit from above;
make my heart with yours accord;
make me feel as you have felt;
make my soul to grow and melt
with the love of Christ my Lord.

Holy Mother, pierce me through;
in my heart each wound renew
of my Savior crucified.
Let me share with you his pain,
who for all my sins was slain,
who for me in torments died. . . .
Christ, when you shall call me hence,
be your mother my defense,
be your cross my victory.
While my body here decays,
may my soul your goodness praise,
safe in paradise with thee. Amen.

Chapter 12 | PRAYERS TO THE SAINTS

Prayers to a Guardian Angel

For he will command his angels concerning you
    to guard you in all your ways.

                       —Psalm 91:11

    O angel of God, my guardian, by the divine goodness I
am entrusted to your charge. Enlighten, keep, govern, and
direct me this day/night/hour.

    Almighty and everlasting God, who has created me in
your own image, and who has deputized your holy angel
to be my guardian, grant me, by his guidance and protection, successfully to pass through all dangers of soul and
body, and, when this life is ended, to enjoy eternal happiness with him, through Jesus Christ our Lord. Amen.

Angel of God, my guardian dear,
to whom his love commits me here,
ever this day be at my side,
to light and guard, to rule and guide.

Prayer to St. Joseph

St. Joseph, the good and faithful servant to whom God committed the care of his family, God's appointed guardian and protector of the life of Jesus, the comfort and support of his holy mother, and co-partner in God's great design of the redemption of mankind, model and patron of pure souls, humble, patient, and reserved, be moved with the confidence we place in your intercession, and accept with kindness this testimony of devotion.

We thank God for the favors he conferred on you, and by your intercession we ask God to make us imitate your virtues. Pray for us, St. Joseph, and obtain for us the happiness of living and dying in the love of Jesus and Mary. Amen.

Prayer to St. Joseph for Our Children

You, who faithfully attended the Holy Child placed in your care, watch over our children, protect them from danger, guard their hearts and minds, walk with them on the path to maturity. Amen.

Prayer to St. Michael the Archangel

St. Michael, glorious prince, chief and champion of the heavenly host, guardian of our souls, conqueror of the rebel angels, steward of the palace of God under Jesus Christ: Keep us free from every ill, from all harm and by your incomparable protection enable us this day and every day to faithfully serve our God. Pray for us, most blessed Michael, prince of the church of Jesus Christ. Amen.

Prayer to St. Michael for Aid

St. Michael the Archangel,
defend us in battle.
Be our defense against the wickedness and snares of
    the devil.
May God rebuke him, we humbly pray,
and do thou,
O Prince of the heavenly hosts,
by the power of God,
thrust into hell Satan,
and all the evil spirits,
who prowl about the world
seeking the ruin of souls. Amen.

Prayer to St. Patrick

O blessed apostle of Ireland, St. Patrick, who became the father and benefactor of that land, receive my prayers. You were the channel of the greatest graces; become also the channel of my thanksgivings to God for having granted me the gift of faith. O blessed father, do not despise my weakness. The cries of children were your mysterious invitation to serve God. Listen then to my humble supplications. . . . I humbly beg your blessing and your particular intercession for obtaining whatever grace you see as necessary for me. Amen.

Prayer to St. Peter at the Eucharist

St. Peter, prince of the apostles, who confessed Christ to be the Son of the living God, not by human instinct but by the revelation of the Father in heaven, who received from Jesus the charge to feed his sheep and also the keys of heaven—pray for me, that in this sacrament I may with steadfast faith and reverence confess my true God and Lord, Jesus Christ, and acknowledge him to be truly present. Amen.

Prayer to St. Teresa

O blessed Teresa, faithful teacher of the art of loving God above all things, through your intercession and by the celestial lights with which God filled your happy mind, obtain for me grace that I may imitate your virtues. Pray for me, as you had a sincere love for Jesus, and as Jesus always loved you. Obtain for me the incomparable advantage of living faithfully and of dying in Jesus' divine love. Amen.

Prayer to St. Vincent de Paul

O glorious St. Vincent, heavenly patron of all associations of charity and father of all the suffering, behold our afflictions and come to our aid. Obtain from our Lord help for the poor, relief for the sick, consolation for the afflicted, protection for the abandoned, charity for the rich, conversion for sinners, zeal for priests, peace for the church, tranquility for the people, salvation for all. Let all experience the effects of your merciful intercession, that they may be united with you above, where there will be neither sorrow, nor weeping, nor pain, but eternal gladness, joy, and happiness. Amen.

Prayer to All the Saints

O Lord, we pray that all your saints may everywhere help us and gladden us by their intercession, that while we celebrate their merits, we may experience their patronage. Grant us peace in our time. Cleanse all iniquity from your church. Prosper the way, the wills, and the actions of us and of all your servants, to the attainment of salvation. Bless our benefactors, and give eternal rest to all the faithful departed. Through your Son Jesus Christ our Lord. Amen.

The Litany of the Saints

This litany, part of the Easter vigil service, can also be used in private devotions.

Lord, have mercy on us. **Lord, have mercy on us.**
Christ, have mercy on us. **Christ, have mercy on us.**
Lord, have mercy on us. **Lord, have mercy on us.**
Christ, hear us. **Christ, graciously hear us.**
God the Father of heaven, **have mercy on us.**
God the Son, Redeemer of the world, **have mercy on us.**
God the Holy Spirit, **have mercy on us.**

Holy Trinity, one God, **have mercy on us.**

Holy Mary, **pray for us.**

Holy Mother of God, **pray for us.**

Holy Virgin of virgins, **pray for us.**

St. Michael, **pray for us.**

St. Gabriel, **pray for us.**

St. Raphael, **pray for us.**

All holy angels and archangels, **pray for us.**

All holy orders of blessed spirits, **pray for us.**

St. John the Baptist, **pray for us.**

St. Joseph, **pray for us.**

All holy patriarchs and prophets, **pray for us.**

St. Peter, **pray for us.**

St. Paul, **pray for us.**

St. Andrew, **pray for us.**

St. James, **pray for us.**

St. John, **pray for us.**

St. Thomas, **pray for us.**

St. James, **pray for us.**

St. Philip, **pray for us.**

St. Bartholomew, **pray for us.**

St. Matthew, **pray for us.**

St. Simon, **pray for us.**

St. Thaddeus, **pray for us.**

St. Matthias, **pray for us.**

St. Barnabas, **pray for us.**

St. Luke, **pray for us.**

St. Mark, **pray for us.**

All holy apostles and evangelists, **pray for us.**

All holy disciples of our Lord, **pray for us.**

All holy innocents, **pray for us.**

St. Stephen, **pray for us.**

St. Lawrence, **pray for us.**

St. Vincent, **pray for us.**

Sts. Fabian and Sebastian, **pray for us.**

Sts. Paul and John, **pray for us.**

Sts. Cosmas and Damian, **pray for us.**

Sts. Gervase and Protase, **pray for us.**

All holy martyrs, **pray for us.**

St. Sylvester, **pray for us.**

St. Gregory, **pray for us.**

St. Ambrose, **pray for us.**

St. Augustine, **pray for us.**

St. Jerome, **pray for us.**

St. Martin, **pray for us.**

St. Nicholas, **pray for us.**

All holy bishops and confessors, **pray for us.**

All holy doctors, **pray for us.**

St. Anthony, **pray for us.**

St. Benedict, **pray for us.**

St. Bernard, **pray for us.**

St. Dominic, **pray for us.**

St. Francis, **pray for us.**

All holy priests and Levites, **pray for us.**

All holy monks and hermits, **pray for us.**

St. Mary Magdalene, **pray for us.**

St. Agatha, **pray for us.**

St. Lucy, **pray for us.**

St. Agnes, **pray for us.**

St. Cecily, **pray for us.**

St. Catharine, **pray for us.**

St. Anastasia, **pray for us.**

All holy virgins and widows, **pray for us.**

All men and women, saints of God,
   make intercession for us.

Be merciful to us, **spare us, O Lord.**

Be merciful to us, **graciously hear us, O Lord.**

From all evil, **O Lord, deliver us.**

From all sin, **O Lord, deliver us.**

From your wrath, **O Lord, deliver us.**

From a sudden and unprovided death,
   O Lord, deliver us.

From the deceits of the devil, **O Lord, deliver us.**

From anger, hatred, and all ill-will,

    O Lord, deliver us.

From the spirit of fornication, **O Lord, deliver us.**

From lightning and tempest, **O Lord, deliver us.**

From everlasting death, **O Lord, deliver us.**

Through the mystery of your holy incarnation,

    O Lord, deliver us.

Through your coming, **O Lord, deliver us.**

Through your nativity, **O Lord, deliver us.**

Through your baptism and holy fasting,

    O Lord, deliver us.

Through your cross and passion,

    O Lord, deliver us.

Through your death and burial,

    O Lord, deliver us.

Through your holy resurrection,

    O Lord, deliver us.

Through your admirable ascension,

    O Lord, deliver us.

Through the coming of the Holy Spirit, the Comforter,

    O Lord, deliver us.

In the day of judgment, **O Lord, deliver us.**

We sinners beseech you to hear us.

That you would spare us, **we beseech you, hear us.**

That you would pardon us, **we beseech you, hear us.**

That you would bring us to true penance,
   we beseech you, hear us.

That you would govern and preserve your holy church,
   we beseech you, hear us.

That you would preserve our apostolic prelate and all
   ecclesiastical orders in holy religion,
   we beseech you, hear us.

That you would humble the enemies of the holy church,
   we beseech you, hear us.

That you would give peace and true concord to Christian
   kings and princes,
   we beseech you, hear us.

That you would grant peace and unity to all Christian
   people,
   we beseech you, hear us.

That you would confirm and preserve us in your holy
   service,
   we beseech you, hear us.

That you would lift up our minds to heavenly desires,
   we beseech you, hear us.

That you would give eternal good things to all our
 benefactors,
 we beseech you, hear us.
That you would deliver our souls and those of our
 brethren, kinsfolk, and benefactors from eternal
 damnation,
 we beseech you, hear us.
That you would give and preserve the fruits of the earth,
 we beseech you, hear us.
That you would give eternal rest to all the faithful
 departed,
 we beseech you, hear us.
That you would graciously hear us,
 we beseech you, hear us.
Son of God, **we beseech you, hear us.**
Lamb of God, who takes away the sins of the world,
 spare us, O Lord.
Lamb of God, who takes away the sins of the world,
 graciously hear us, O Lord.
Lamb of God, who takes away the sins of the world,
 have mercy on us.
Christ, hear us. Christ, **graciously hear us.**
Lord, have mercy on us. **Christ, have mercy on us.**
Lord, have mercy on us.

PART 4

CLASSIC DEVOTIONAL PRAYERS

May the power of your cross, O Christ, be shown to be greater than the author of sin.

—Blessed Pope John Paul II

In the Garden of Gethsemane, Jesus asked his sleepy disciples if they could please wait and watch and pray with him in his distress. Later, at Jesus' arrest, those same disciples scattered. In later centuries Christians took great pains to try to "be with" Jesus in his final hours. To place themselves in the passion setting, pilgrims walked the Via Dolorosa in the streets of Jerusalem. Those who could not make the trip would symbolically follow the way of the cross, a pattern of prayer that has become standardized to commemorate fourteen distinct moments from Jesus' conviction to his burial. Here in this section we present prayers to help focus your meditations on the Stations of the Cross.

We also include a Litany to the Holy Spirit, which is condensed from a seventeenth-century prayer by James Merlo

Horstius and based on scriptural descriptions of the Spirit's role and work. A litany is another classic form of Catholic prayer, in which God or a saint is addressed by various names or attributes. When a litany is prayed communally, a leader says the invocations and the people respond with the specific, repeated intercession, such as "have mercy on us" or "hear our prayer." A litany can also be prayed privately, possibly as a novena—nine days of prayer asking for divine help for daily concerns or special intentions.

The Rosary is an ancient form of devotional prayer that combines meditation and vocalization with the physical component—fingering the beads. The repetitious nature of this ancient prayer can be very comforting in times of distress.

Chapter 13 | THE STATIONS OF THE CROSS

From the early days of Christianity, followers of Christ visited sites in Jerusalem that commemorated aspects of Jesus' passion—his suffering and death. In later centuries pilgrims returning to Europe built representational stations, reminding them of the principal events on Jesus' way to Calvary. The Franciscans set a tradition of fourteen "stations," at which reflective prayers are said. The popular devotion, often called "the Way of the Cross," allows us to make the journey in spirit to Calvary, identifying with our Lord's sufferings and asking for his mercy. During Lent many parishes hold communal celebrations of the Way of the Cross. But individuals may pray the Stations of the Cross privately either at home or at church before representations of each event on Christ's journey to Calvary

Preparing to Pray

O Jesus, infinitely good and merciful, I fly to the arms of your mercy. My sin has offended you. I repent and implore your grace, which burns away the impurities as it melts my heart and converts my being.

With sincere intent to amend my life, and in memory of that painful journey you traveled for our redemption to the cross of Calvary, I begin this devotion—under your sacred protection and in imitation of your merciful mother. Let this holy exercise obtain for me mercy in this life and glory in the next. Amen.

Station 1
Jesus is condemned to death by Pilate.

We adore you, Christ, and bless you.

Because by your holy cross you have redeemed the world.

Consider the court scene at which Pilate condemns the Lord to death. Having been beaten and mocked, Jesus' pointed words, "You would have no power over me unless it had been given you from above" reveal his awareness of a divine plan set in motion by Pilate's decision (see John 19:9-11).

Lord, I have deserved this sentence of death, yet you died for me that I might live for you.

Our Father . . .
Hail Mary . . .
Glory be to the Father . . .
Have mercy on us, O Lord. Have mercy on us.

Station 2
Jesus takes the cross on his shoulder.

We adore you, Christ, and bless you.
Because by your holy cross you have redeemed the world.

Consider the scene as soldiers lay the wooden cross on Jesus' bleeding shoulders.

Lord Jesus, my sin loaded your shoulders with the heavy burden of the cross. But so often I run from even the appearance of mortification or discomfort. Lord Christ, lay on my neck the cross of true penance. For love of you, let me bear the adversities of this life and cling to you in the bonds of love. Any cross you ask me to bear is meant to conduct me not to a Calvary of crucifixion, but ultimately to the joys of eternal glory.

Our Father . . .
Hail Mary . . .
Glory be to the Father . . .
Have mercy on us, O Lord. Have mercy on us.

Station 3

Jesus falls the first time under the weight of the cross.

We adore you, Christ, and bless you.
Because by your holy cross you have redeemed the world.

Consider the moment when Jesus stumbles, the burden of the cross and our sin pushing him to the limits of his endurance.

O Jesus, stretch your holy hand to me, to pick me up when I fall into sin. And prevent me from committing mortal sin; so that at the hour of my death, I may secure the salvation you won for me by your sacrificial death.

Our Father . . .
Hail Mary . . .
Glory be to the Father . . .
Have mercy on us, O Lord. Have mercy on us.

Station 4

Jesus meets his sorrowful mother.

We adore you, Christ, and bless you.
Because by your holy cross you have redeemed the world.

Consider the moment when Jesus sees his mother in the crowd. The look exchanged between them is a heart-breaking grace to them both. It's as if their tears mingle, mother and son each silently speaking courage and strength to overcome despair.

Lord Christ, by the heart-broken compassion of your faithful mother, grant me the grace of perseverance. O Mary, Refuge of Sinners, intercede for me on this my journey and also at the hour of my death.

Our Father . . .
Hail Mary . . .
Glory be to the Father . . .
Have mercy on us, O Lord. Have mercy on us.

Station 5
Simon of Cyrene helps Jesus carry his cross.

We adore you, Christ, and bless you.
Because by your holy cross you have redeemed the world.

Consider the encounter—when the soldiers compel a bystander to participate in Jesus' sufferings by carrying the cross when Jesus can no longer do so. Jesus' physical relief is only temporary, as he faces greater torments. It's not clear that Simon carries the cross willingly; nevertheless he picks up the burden and joins Jesus on the way of sorrows.

Lord, give me the grace to accompany you to Mount Calvary. I want to share in your suffering and carry your cross willingly, even cheerfully, but I cannot do so without the mercy and strength that is mine because of your resurrection power.

Our Father . . .
Hail Mary . . .
Glory be to the Father . . .
Have mercy on us, O Lord. Have mercy on us.

Station 6

Veronica wipes the face of Christ with her veil.

We adore you, Christ, and bless you.
Because by your holy cross you have redeemed the world.

Consider the act of mercy of St. Veronica, who steps out from the crowd and wipes the sweat and blood from Jesus' face—the image of which remains imprinted on her veil. Though we cannot personally wipe the face of our Lord, we can wipe the tear of wretchedness from the eye of misery, wherever we find it.

Lord, stamp your image on my soul, so that I may love you wholeheartedly and love others in and by the power of your love.

Our Father . . .
Hail Mary . . .
Glory be to the Father . . .
Have mercy on us, O Lord. Have mercy on us.

Station 7

Jesus falls under the cross a second time.

We adore you, Christ, and bless you.
Because by your holy cross you have redeemed the world.

Consider the scene of Jesus stumbling again on his road to the cross. Do my own besetting sins and destructive compulsions contribute to his second fall?

Lord, you are with me in my failings, even as you offer me the grace and strength to persevere and take the next step toward repentance and redemption. I humbly ask your mercy in my time of weakness and thank you for your eternal faithfulness.

Our Father . . .
Hail Mary . . .
Glory be to the Father . . .
Have mercy on us, O Lord. Have mercy on us.

Station 8

Jesus consoles the women of Jerusalem,
who weep for him.

We adore you, Christ, and bless you.
Because by your holy cross you have redeemed the world.

Consider the group of mourners who follow the pitiable procession to Calvary. Jesus speaks to the women, addressing their own vulnerabilities and mortality: "Daughters of Jerusalem, do not weep for me, but weep for yourselves and for your children" (Luke 23:28).

Lord, I weep with you—as you weep with me—for my own sin and the way evil and its destructiveness have ravaged the world, throughout history, to this very day. I pray for the coming of your kingdom, where every tear will be dried, when our full redemption will be realized.

Our Father . . .
Hail Mary . . .
Glory be to the Father . . .
Have mercy on us, O Lord. Have mercy on us.

Station 9

Jesus falls under the cross a third time.

We adore you, Christ, and bless you.

Because by your holy cross you have redeemed the world.

Consider Jesus, falling a third time, at the foot of Mount Calvary, as he is mercilessly spurred on by his executioners.

Lord, with you I cry out against the injustice I see in the world. Forgive me for the suffering I cause you; for the pain I inflict, knowingly or unknowingly, on my brothers and sisters, each a beloved soul for whom you suffered and died.

Our Father . . .

Hail Mary . . .

Glory be to the Father . . .

Have mercy on us, O Lord. Have mercy on us.

Station 10
Jesus is stripped of his garments.

We adore you, Christ, and bless you.
Because by your holy cross you have redeemed the world.

Consider the soldiers' humiliating act of stripping Jesus of his clothing, the covering that has represented physical dignity since our first ancestors' first sin and its attendant self-conscious shame.

Sinless Savior, you were willing to be mortified on my behalf, stripped of your belongings and symbols of personal identity. In my sin I stand with you, stripped of my pride. I let go of my worldly attachments, so that I cling only to my identity in you.

Our Father . . .
Hail Mary . . .
Glory be to the Father . . .
Have mercy on us, O Lord. Have mercy on us.

Station 11
Jesus is nailed to the cross.

We adore you, Christ, and bless you.
Because by your holy cross you have redeemed the world.

Consider the action of the soldiers nailing Jesus' hands and feet to the wooden cross. They turn the cross upright and set it into the ground. Torturously hanging between life and death, Jesus gasps for breath, as his friends and enemies watch on.

Jesus, Lamb of God, as you were nailed to the wood of the cross to free me of my sins, so I confess my sins to you, my Redeemer. By your wounds I am healed (see 1 Peter 2:24).

Our Father . . .
Hail Mary . . .
Glory be to the Father . . .
Have mercy on us, O Lord. Have mercy on us.

Station 12
Jesus dies on the cross.

We adore you, Christ, and bless you.
Because by your holy cross you have redeemed the world.

Consider the scene as Jesus forgives his enemies, commends his spirit into the hands of his Father, and declares, "It is finished" (John 19:30). He then breathes his last and expires. At that hour the veil in the temple is miraculously torn from top to bottom, announcing that Christ has launched the kingdom of God. Heaven and earth quake at the tragedy that is also a triumph.

Lord, you could have called down angels to spare yourself, but instead you willingly died to deliver us from eternal captivity. In gratitude may I die daily to the sins that grieve you and live in the triumph of your finished act of redemption.

Our Father . . .
Hail Mary . . .
Glory be to the Father . . .
Have mercy on us, O Lord. Have mercy on us.

Station 13

Jesus is taken down from the cross.

We adore you, Christ, and bless you.
Because by your holy cross you have redeemed the
world.

Consider the respectful and gracious act of Joseph of
Arimathea and Nicodemus. They take Jesus' tortured
body from the cross and place it in the arms of Mary, who
lovingly mourns for the loss of her lifeless son.

Lord, count me among the disciples who cared for you
with tender respect. Mary, I ask you to open your arms to
enfold me in my hour of need; care for me when I cannot
help myself; intercede on my behalf, now and at the time
of my death.

Our Father . . .
Hail Mary . . .
Glory be to the Father . . .
Have mercy on us, O Lord. Have mercy on us.

Station 14
Jesus is laid in the tomb.

We adore you, Christ, and bless you.
Because by your holy cross you have redeemed the world.

Consider the scene at the holy sepulchre, where Jesus' body is laid to rest by Joseph and Nicodemus, accompanied by Mary. They lay out the body and watch soldiers seal the tomb. They do not realize that the entombment will be temporary; they do not know what Easter morning will mean for them or for us.

Resurrected Lord, entomb yourself in my heart, so that I can live every day in full service to you and your kingdom.

Our Father . . .
Hail Mary . . .
Glory be to the Father . . .
Have mercy on us, O Lord. Have mercy on us.

Closing Prayer

Loving Jesus, for my salvation you traveled the painful journey to the cross. Let me follow the footsteps marked by you, the path marked with blood and the pain it represents, through the streets of Jerusalem. Accept with mercy this devotion I've performed in honor of your passion and death. Accept it for the salvation of the living and the repose of the faithful departed. Have mercy, O Lord. Amen.

Chapter 14 | LITANY TO THE HOLY SPIRIT

God, the Father of heaven, **have mercy on us.**

God the Son, Redeemer of the world, **have mercy on us.**

God the Holy Spirit, **have mercy on us.**

Holy Trinity, one God, **have mercy on us.**

Spirit, who proceeded from the Father and the Son,
  have mercy on us.

Spirit of truth, who brings all things to our mind,
  have mercy on us.

Spirit, who teaches us all truth, **have mercy on us.**

Spirit, who overshadowed Mary, **have mercy on us.**

Spirit, by whose power the Son became incarnate,
  have mercy on us.

Spirit, who descended on the apostles at Pentecost,
  have mercy on us.

Spirit of God, who dwells in us, **have mercy on us.**

Spirit of wisdom and understanding, **have mercy on us.**

Spirit of counsel and of courage, **have mercy on us.**

Spirit of knowledge and of godliness, **have mercy on us.**

Spirit of grace and mercy, **have mercy on us.**

Spirit of sanctification, **have mercy on us.**

Spirit of power, of love, and of sobriety,
  have mercy on us.

Spirit, by whose inspiration spoke the holy men of God,
have mercy on us.

Spirit, who distributes God's gifts and graces,
have mercy on us.

Spirit, who prays for us, **have mercy on us.**

Spirit, by whom we are born again,
have mercy on us.

Spirit, who helps us in our infirmities,
have mercy on us.

Spirit, who quickens and strengthens us,
have mercy on us.

Spirit, the Paraclete, who abides with us forever,
have mercy on us.

Be favorable, O Holy Spirit, **and spare us.**

Be favorable, O Holy Spirit, **and hear us.**

From all evil, **deliver us, O Holy Spirit.**

From the temptations and snares of the devil,
deliver us, O Holy Spirit.

From all presumption and desperation,
deliver us, O Holy Spirit.

We pray that you would hear us and spare us,

That as we live in the Spirit, so we may also walk in
the Spirit,
hear us, we pray.

That we may be careful to keep the unity of the Spirit
in the bond of peace,
hear us, we pray.
That as temples of the Holy Spirit, we may beware
of violating our bodies,
hear us, we pray.
That you would make us hunger and thirst after true
justice,
hear us, we pray.
That you would pour into us sincere love and desire
for mercy,
hear us, we pray.
Lamb of God, who takes away the sins of the world,
pour out upon us the Holy Spirit.
Lamb of God, who takes away the sins of the world,
send forth upon us the promised Spirit of the Father.
Lamb of God, who takes away the sins of the world,
give us the Spirit of peace.

Our Father . . .
Hail Mary . . .

Let us pray: O God to whom every heart is open,
every desire known, and from whom no secret is hid,

purify the thoughts of our hearts by the inspiration of the Holy Spirit, that we may perfectly love you and worthily praise you.

Let the power of the Holy Spirit be with us, we pray, both graciously to purify our hearts and to defend us from all adversities.

Almighty and everlasting God, by whose Spirit the whole body of the church is sanctified and governed, hear our supplications, that by the gift of your grace we may faithfully serve you, through Jesus Christ, our Lord. Amen.

Chapter 15 | THE ROSARY

The Rosary is an ancient set of repeated prayers, during which the one praying meditates on events in the lives of Jesus and Mary. In this way, the Rosary is a summary and review of the gospel. Traditionally there were fifteen mysteries—three groupings of five (Joyful Mysteries, Sorrowful Mysteries, Glorious Mysteries). Pope John Paul II added a fourth set of Luminous Mysteries representing Jesus' three years of earthly ministry.

Fingering a set of rosary beads helps the pray-er count the repetitive lines and stay focused.

After making the sign of the cross, with the crucifix in your palm, say the Apostles' Creed. Fingering the first large bead, say one Our Father. On each of the three smaller beads say one Hail Mary (representing the virtues of faith, hope, and charity). On the thread or chain before the second large bead repeat one Glory Be to the Father.

On the large bead name and reflect on the first Joyful Mystery (see below) and repeat one Our Father. The long, circular chain is divided into five "decades" or sections of ten small beads, followed by a large bead. On each of the ten small beads, say one Hail Mary. On the thread or chain before the large bead repeat one Glory Be (*Gloria Patri*).

While fingering this same next large bead, proceed to the second Joyful Mystery, saying one Our Father, followed by ten Hail Marys on the ten small beads. . . .

When you have prayed through all five Joyful Mysteries, your fingers are back at the crucifix juncture. To pray an entire Rosary, pray around the beads again, reflecting now on the Luminous Mysteries, then the Sorrowful, and finally a "Glorious" round.

But you needn't pray the entire rosary in one sitting. One form recommends praying the Joyful Mysteries on Mondays and Saturdays; and also on Sundays, from Advent through the beginning of Lent. The Luminous Mysteries are often prayed on Thursdays. The Sorrowful Mysteries are traditionally prayed on Tuesdays and Fridays and on the Sundays in Lent. The Glorious Mysteries are traditionally prayed on Wednesdays; and also on Sundays from Easter through Advent.

The Joyful Mysteries

1. The Annunciation (Luke 1:26-38)

Contemplate the mystery of how the angel Gabriel saluted Mary with the title "Full of Grace" and told her she had been chosen to bear the incarnate Son of God.

Our Father (one time). Hail Mary (ten times). Glory Be to the Father (one time).

2. The Visitation (Luke 1:39-56)

Contemplate the mystery of how Mary journeyed to visit her cousin Elizabeth, who had conceived in her old age. Elizabeth's unborn child leapt for joy at Mary's arrival and Elizabeth exclaimed, "Blessed are you among women, and blessed is the fruit of your womb."

Our Father (one time). Hail Mary (ten times). Glory Be to the Father (one time).

3. The Nativity (Luke 2:1-19)

Contemplate the mystery of how Mary brought forth her Son, our redeemer, and laid him in a manger, because there was no room for him in the Bethlehem inns. That night angels announced the good news to poor shepherds, who came to worship the Christ child.

Our Father (one time). Hail Mary (ten times). Glory Be to the Father (one time).

4. The Presentation (Luke 2:22-40)

Contemplate the mystery of how Mary, on the day of her purification, presented the infant Jesus in the temple, where holy Simeon and Anna recognized the Christ child and thanked God for his mercy.

Our Father (one time). Hail Mary (ten times). Glory Be to the Father (one time).

5. The Finding of Jesus in the Temple (Luke 2:41-52)

Contemplate the mystery of how Mary and Joseph lost twelve-year-old Jesus in Jerusalem, but after three days found him in the temple, engaged in his "Father's business," expounding the Scriptures with learned rabbis.

Our Father (one time). Hail Mary (ten times). Glory Be to the Father (one time).

The Luminous Mysteries

1. The Baptism of Our Lord (Matthew 3:13-17)

Contemplate the mystery of how at our Lord's baptism in the Jordan he saw the Spirit of God descending upon him like a dove; and a voice declared, "This is my beloved Son in whom I am well pleased."

Our Father (one time). Hail Mary (ten times). Glory Be to the Father (one time).

2. The Manifestation of Jesus at Cana (John 2:1-11)

Contemplate the mystery of how Jesus performed his first miracle by turning water into wine for wedding guests at Cana.

Our Father (one time). Hail Mary (ten times). Glory Be to the Father (one time).

3. The Proclamation of the Kingdom (Mark 1:14-20)

Contemplate the mystery of how Jesus announced that he had come to launch the kingdom of God, bringing salvation, healing, and deliverance from evil for all.

Our Father (one time). Hail Mary (ten times). Glory Be to the Father (one time).

4. The Transfiguration of Jesus (Luke 9:28-36)

Contemplate the mystery of how on the mountainside some disciples saw Jesus' transfigured glory as he spoke about his death and resurrection with Elijah and Moses.

Our Father (one time). Hail Mary (ten times). Glory Be to the Father (one time).

5. The Institution of the Eucharist (Mark 14:22-25)

Contemplate the mystery of how Jesus at the Passover feast the night before his death, took bread and wine and declared, "This is my body; this is my blood," commanding his disciples to continue celebrating this eucharistic feast throughout the coming ages.

Our Father (one time). Hail Mary (ten times). Glory Be to the Father (one time).

The Sorrowful (Dolorous) Mysteries

1. The Agonizing Prayer in the Garden (Luke 22:39-46)

Contemplate the mystery of how Jesus in the Garden of Gethsemane was so afflicted on our behalf that he was sweating drops of blood. "Not my will but yours," he prayed.

Our Father (one time). Hail Mary (ten times). Glory Be to the Father (one time).

2. The Scourging of Jesus (John 19:1-3)

Contemplate the mystery of how Jesus was cruelly bound to a pillar and scourged at Pilate's house. Consider the mystery prophesied in Isaiah—that by his stripes we are healed (see Isaiah 53:5).

Our Father (one time). Hail Mary (ten times). Glory Be to the Father (one time).

3. The Crowning with Thorns (Matthew 27:27-31)

Contemplate the mystery of how Jesus was mocked as king of the Jews by those who bloodied his brow with a crown of thorns and placed a purple robe over his shoulders.

Our Father (one time). Hail Mary (ten times). Glory Be to the Father (one time).

4. The Carrying of the Cross (Matthew 27:32)

Contemplate the mystery of how Jesus, being sentenced to die, patiently bore the wooden cross through the streets of Jerusalem to his hill of execution.

Our Father (one time). Hail Mary (ten times). Glory Be to the Father (one time).

5. The Crucifixion (Matthew 27:35-50)

Contemplate the mystery of how our Lord on Mount Calvary was nailed to a cross and died in the presence of his distressed mother.

Our Father (one time). Hail Mary (ten times). Glory Be to the Father (one time).

The Glorious Mysteries

1. The Resurrection (Mark 16:1-14)

Contemplate the mystery of how our Lord, Jesus Christ, triumphing gloriously over death, arose from the grave on the third day.

Our Father (one time). Hail Mary (ten times). Glory Be to the Father (one time).

2. The Ascension (Luke 24:44-53)

Contemplate the mystery of how our Lord, Jesus Christ, forty days after his resurrection, ascended into heaven in the sight of his mother and his apostles, to their great joy.

Our Father (one time). Hail Mary (ten times). Glory Be to the Father (one time).

3. The Descent of the Holy Spirit (Acts 2:1-12)

Contemplate the mystery of how our Lord, Jesus Christ, sent the promised Holy Spirit upon his apostles and his mother, to empower them for service and ministry.

Our Father (one time). Hail Mary (ten times). Glory Be to the Father (one time).

4. The Assumption of Mary (See the assumption of Elijah—2 Kings 2:11)

Contemplate the mystery of how the blessed Virgin, at the time of her death, was assumed, body and soul, into heaven, accompanied by the holy angels.

Our Father (one time). Hail Mary (ten times). Glory Be to the Father (one time).

5. The Crowning of the Blessed Virgin Mary (Revelation 12)

Contemplate the mystery of how the glorious Virgin Mary was crowed queen of heaven by her Son.

Our Father (one time). Hail Mary (ten times). Glory Be to the Father (one time).

The Rosary ends with the following prayer:

Hail, Holy Queen
(Salve Regina)

Hail, holy Queen, Mother of Mercy, our life, our sweetness, and our hope. To you do we cry, poor banished children of Eve. To you do we send up our sighs, mourning and weeping in this valley of tears. Turn, then, most gracious advocate, your eyes of mercy toward us, and after this, our exile, show unto us the blessed fruit of your womb, Jesus, O clement, O loving, O sweet virgin Mary.

Pray for us, O Holy Mother of God.

That we may be made worthy of the promises of Christ.

Let us pray. O God, whose only begotten Son, by his life, death, and resurrection, has purchased for us the rewards of eternal life, grant, we pray, that by meditating upon these mysteries of the most holy rosary of the Blessed Virgin Mary, we may imitate what they contain and obtain what they promise, through the same Christ, our Lord. Amen.

The Rosary is sometimes followed by the Litany of Loreto.

The Litany of Loreto

Lord, have mercy. **Lord, have mercy.**
Christ, have mercy. **Christ, have mercy.**
Lord, have mercy. **Lord, have mercy.**
Christ, hear us. **Christ, graciously hear us.**
God, the Father of heaven, **have mercy on us.**
God the Son, Redeemer of the world, **have mercy on us.**
God the Holy Spirit, **have mercy on us.**

Holy Trinity, one God, **have mercy on us.**
Holy Mary, **pray for us.**
Holy Mother of God, **pray for us.**
Holy Virgin of virgins, **pray for us.**
Mother of Christ, **pray for us.**
Mother of divine grace, **pray for us.**
Mother most pure, **pray for us.**
Mother most chaste, **pray for us.**
Mother inviolate, **pray for us.**
Mother undefiled, **pray for us.**
Mother most amiable, **pray for us.**
Mother most admirable, **pray for us.**
Mother of our Creator, **pray for us.**
Mother of our Savior, **pray for us.**
Virgin most prudent, **pray for us.**
Virgin most venerable, **pray for us.**
Virgin most renowned, **pray for us.**
Virgin most powerful, **pray for us.**
Virgin most merciful, **pray for us.**
Virgin most faithful, **pray for us.**
Mirror of justice, **pray for us.**
Seat of wisdom, **pray for us.**
Cause of our joy, **pray for us.**
Spiritual vessel, **pray for us.**

Vessel of honor, **pray for us.**

Singular vessel of devotion, **pray for us.**

Mystical rose, **pray for us.**

Tower of David, **pray for us.**

Tower of ivory, **pray for us.**

House of gold, **pray for us.**

Ark of the covenant, **pray for us.**

Gate of heaven, **pray for us.**

Morning star, **pray for us.**

Health of the sick, **pray for us.**

Refuge of sinners, **pray for us.**

Comforter of the afflicted, **pray for us.**

Help of Christians, **pray for us.**

Queen of angels, **pray for us.**

Queen of patriarchs, **pray for us.**

Queen of prophets, **pray for us.**

Queen of apostles, **pray for us.**

Queen of martyrs, **pray for us.**

Queen of confessors, **pray for us.**

Queen of virgins, **pray for us.**

Queen of all saints, **pray for us.**

Queen conceived without original sin, **pray for us.**

Queen assumed into heaven, **pray for us.**

Queen of the most holy Rosary, **pray for us.**

Lamb of God, who takes away the sins of the world,
spare us, O Lord.
Lamb of God, who takes away the sins of the world,
graciously hear us, O Lord.
Lamb of God, who takes away the sins of the world,
have mercy on us.
Pray for us, O holy Mother of God.
**That we may be made worthy of the promises of
Christ.**

Let us pray. Pour forth, O Lord, your divine grace into
our hearts, that we to whom the incarnation of Christ
your Son was made known by the message of an angel,
may by his passion and cross be brought to the glory of
his resurrection, through the same Christ our Lord. **Amen.**

PART 5

PRAYERS FOR
SPECIAL NEEDS

I thank my God every time I remember you,
constantly praying with joy in every one of my prayers
for all of you, because of your sharing in the gospel from
the first day until now. . . . This is my prayer, that your
love may overflow more and more with knowledge and
full insight to help you to determine what is best, so that
in the day of Christ you may be pure and blameless,
having produced the harvest of righteousness that comes
through Jesus Christ for the glory and praise of God.
—Philippians 1:3-11

As this Philippians passage makes clear, praying for others, whether as individuals or as groups, is deeply rooted in the biblical tradition. Here, in this final section, we offer a selection of traditional prayers as well as new prayers, written by Bob French (BF) especially for this collection. We pray for nourishment, virtues, and stamina—strength to live a life pleasing to God. We pray for our spiritual leaders, our country, our loved ones, those who are suffering or facing death. . . . But we also pray that God will oversee and bring good from specific occasions. And we pray that God's kingdom will be made known, even through the distressing and turbulent times that we face in this first century of the new millennium. The God who is the keeper of time will guard and guide us through even these perilous times.

Chapter 16 | PRAYERS FOR GIFTS AND GRACES

Obtain for Me These Graces

O Father! O Son! O Holy Spirit!

O Holy Trinity! O Jesus! O Mary!

O blessed angels of God!

O saints of paradise, men and women, obtain for me
these graces, which I ask through the precious blood
of Jesus Christ:

To do the holy will of God.

To live in union with God.

To do all for God.

To seek alone God's glory.

To sanctify myself for God alone.

To understand my own nothingness.

To know more and more the will of God.

Lord Jesus, offer your most precious blood to the eternal Father for my poor soul, for the holy souls in purgatory, for the wants of the holy church, for the conversion of sinners, for the whole world. Amen.

A Prayer for Wisdom and Goodness
St. Thomas Aquinas (c. 1225–c. 1275)

Grant me, almighty and merciful God, to desire fervently, to investigate wisely, to acknowledge sincerely, and to fulfill perfectly the things that please you. Give me the knowledge, ability, and will to do what you require of me. And grant me grace to perform it well, to the advancement of my soul's salvation.

Let my way to you be safe, direct, and perfect, not failing either in prosperity or adversity, but leaving me humbled by the one and contented by the other. Let me thank you in prosperity and preserve my patience in adversity. Let me be glad or sorry for nothing, except what carries me on to you or draws me back from you. Let me seek to please, and fear to displease, none but you. . . .

Make me, O my God, humble without pretense, merry without dissipation, sorrowful without dejection, sedate without moroseness, active without levity, truthful without duplicity, timid without despair, hopeful in you without presumption, chaste without taint. . . .

Give me, dearest Lord, the understanding to know you, the diligence to seek you, the wisdom to find you, the conversation to please you, the perseverance to await you, and the confidence happily to embrace you. Grant me by penance to be pierced with your sufferings, and by grace to enjoy your blessings on the way, and by glory at last to possess your delights in my home. Who, with the Father and the Holy Spirit, lives and reigns, God, world without end. Amen.

Day by Day
St. Richard of Chichester (1197–1253)

Day by day,
dear Lord, of you
three things I pray:
to know you more clearly,
love you more dearly,
follow you more nearly, day by day. Amen.

A Prayer in Honor of the Five Wounds

O Lord Jesus Christ! by the five wounds that you were pleased to receive upon the cross for the love of me, help me, your servant whom you have redeemed with your precious blood. Amen.

Jesus, Bless Me

Blood of Jesus, wash me.
Passion of Jesus, strengthen me.
Wounds of Jesus, heal me.
Heart of Jesus, receive me.
Spirit of Jesus, enliven me.
Love of Jesus, inflame me.
Mercy of Jesus, spare me.
Cross of Jesus, support me.
Thorns of Jesus, crown me.
Signs of Jesus, plead for me.
Agony of Jesus, atone for me.
Lips of Jesus, bless me in life and death,
in time and in eternity. Amen.

A Prayer for a New Venture or Season

Omnipotence of the Father, help my weakness and
deliver me from the depths of sadness. Wisdom of the
Son, direct all my thoughts, words, and actions. Love of
the Holy Spirit, be the source and beginning of all the
operations of my soul, so they may always conform to
your divine will. Amen.

Prayer of Dedication
St. Ignatius of Loyola (1491–1556)

Take, O Lord, and receive all my liberty, my memory, my understanding, and my whole will. You have given me all that I am and all that I possess; I surrender it all to you that you may dispose of it according to your will. Give me only your love and your grace; with these I will be rich enough, and will have no more to desire. Amen.

Prayer to the Sacred Heart of Jesus
St. Gertrude (1256–1302)

O Sacred Heart of Jesus, living and quickening source of eternal life, infinite treasury of the divinity, burning furnace of divine love—you are my refuge and my sanctuary. O my loving Savior, consume my heart with that burning fire with which your heart is ever inflamed. Pour down on my soul those graces that flow from your love. Let my heart be so united with yours that our wills may be one—that in all things my will may be conformed to yours, that your will may be the standard and rule of my desires and my actions. Amen.

Grant Us Quiet and Contented Minds
Christina Rossetti (1830–1894)

O Lord, whose way is perfect, help us, we pray, always to trust in your goodness, that walking with you and following you in all simplicity, we may possess quiet and contented minds and may cast all our cares on you, who cares for us. Grant this, O Lord, for your dear Son's sake, Jesus Christ. Amen.

A Prayer for Guidance

Lord, I come to consult you and to ask you for light and direction. Let me know how I am to act. Let me know, by means best known to yourself, how to proceed according to your will. Teach me how to conduct myself and provide the means by which this, my next endeavor, may succeed to your glory and the good welfare of my soul. I offer you a heart prepared to follow your direction, because it is in you that I place all my hopes; I desire nothing more than the accomplishment of your will. Let your divine light shine on me, and do not abandon me to my own darkness. Amen.

Prayer of St. Francis
St. Francis of Assisi (1181–1226)

Lord, make us instruments of your peace. Where there is hatred, let us sow love; where there is injury, pardon; where there is discord, union; where there is doubt, faith; where there is despair, hope; where there is darkness, light; where there is sadness, joy. Grant that we may not so much seek to be consoled as to console; to be understood as to understand; to be loved as to love. For it is in giving that we receive; it is in pardoning that we are pardoned; and it is in dying that we are born to eternal life. Amen.

Father, Give to Your Child . . .

Father, I don't know what I ought to ask. You alone know what I lack; you love me better than I can love myself. Give to your child that which [s]he knows not how to ask. I dare not ask for either crosses or consolations. I only present myself before you. I lay open to you my heart: Consider my needs and act according to your mercies. Strike or cure, raise up or cast down. I adore your divine will without knowing it. I hold my peace. I sacrifice and abandon myself to you. I have no other desire than to accomplish your divine will. Amen.

A Prayer Before Meditation

My God, my creator, my last end, and my all—I believe that you are present, that I am in you, and that you are in me, that your eyes are fixed on me, as if I were the only one in the world. With profound respect I adore you, O my God. I unite my adoration to that of your angels and the saints in heaven and the faithful on earth.

For your glory and for the sanctification of my soul, I meditate on this Scripture reading. I renounce all the distractions that may come, through the levity of my mind or the ploys of the enemy.

Adorable Trinity, Father, Son, and Holy Spirit—I consecrate to you my memory, my understanding, and my will. Grant me the attention, insight, and affections necessary to profit by this meditation. O my most loving Savior, permit me to unite myself to you and to pray in your name. O my blessed Mother, my holy angel, and holy patron saints, assist me. Amen.

Psalm 23

The LORD is my shepherd, I shall not want.

He makes me lie down in green pastures;

he leads me beside still waters;
    he restores my soul.
He leads me in right paths
    for his name's sake.
Even though I walk through the darkest valley,
    I fear no evil;
for you are with me;
    your rod and your staff—
    they comfort me.
You prepare a table before me
    in the presence of my enemies;
you anoint my head with oil;
    my cup overflows.
Surely goodness and mercy shall follow me
    all the days of my life,
and I shall dwell in the house of the Lord
    my whole life long.

Jesus, Music of My Soul

May the adorable name of Jesus be the sweet and daily music of my soul and the seal of my heart. When in the agony and cold sweat of death, I give the last look for mercy, may the parting sigh of my soul be "Jesus." Amen.

Clothe Me with Truth
St. Catherine of Siena (1347–1380)

Clothe me, clothe me with yourself, O eternal Truth, that I may run my mortal course with true obedience and the light of holy faith. Amen.

Psalm 61:1-4

Hear my cry, O God;
    listen to my prayer.
From the end of the earth I call to you,
    when my heart is faint.

Lead me to the rock
    that is higher than I;
for you are my refuge,
    a strong tower against the enemy.
Let me abide in your tent forever,
    find refuge under the shelter of your wings.

Chapter 17 | PRAYERS FOR PARTICULAR PEOPLE AND CIRCUMSTANCES

For the Church

Father, I pray that the church would truly be a reflection of your glory. May we follow your calling to be the light of the world and to carry everywhere the love and compassion of your son, Jesus. May we have the courage to be the salt of the earth and the strength to proclaim your gospel in the face of injustice, oppression, and evil. May we live as one body, united in your Spirit, bearing one another's burdens and helping one another to reach the joys of heaven. Amen. —BF

For the Pope, Bishops, and Clergy

I pray for all your shepherds, Father, that you would provide the strength they need to fulfill their mission. Fill them with your wisdom, Lord, so that they will be effective in reaching the lost, comforting the sorrowful, and rousing the lukewarm. Make them sensitive to your Spirit, so that they will know how to teach, inspire, and guide your church. Give them listening hearts that are responsive to the needs of your people. Bless them and let them know you are always with them. Amen. —BF

For Vocations to Priesthood and Religious Life

Lord, send workers into your harvest! As you summoned the apostles from their nets, you are still summoning men and women from the cares of this world into the service of your kingdom. Open their ears to hear your voice and show them the unlimited possibility of a life surrendered to you as a priest, brother, or sister. Give them the courage to test your calling and the perseverance to see it through. Set their hearts on fire for you, Lord! Amen. —BF

For Discernment of Vocation

Father, in your wisdom you have already marked out a plan for my life; help me to discover it. Send me your light to reveal the specific calling you have given to me, the calling that would bring you the greatest glory and me the greatest joy. Send me your love to answer the call, whatever it may be. I put my hopes and dreams into your hands. Use me as you will, and guide me along the path you have chosen for me. Amen. —BF

For the Conversion of Sinners

Lord Jesus, touch the hearts of all of my loved ones, friends, and acquaintances who do not know you—and every lost soul, from the most desperate to the most indifferent. Pierce them with your love. Break down the walls of unbelief that imprison them, and shatter all the strongholds of Satan that darken their minds and keep them from understanding the truth. May they become new creations, changed forever by your transforming message of salvation. Amen. —BF

For Caregivers

Lord Jesus, give your compassion to those of us who care for the sick and the infirm. Give us your patience with the weaknesses of those we care for and help us to see your face in theirs. Just as we would gladly help you carry your cross, help us to share in the crosses of the weak. Show us the great blessing of emptying ourselves in service to others—especially when we don't feel like it, when our schedules will not allow it, and when we are carrying our own burdens. Make us cheerful givers, Lord! Amen. —BF

For Healing of Others

Father, I know many who are sick right now: family members, friends, and all those far and near whom I've been asked to pray for. I bring each one to the foot of your cross, the source of abundant mercy and healing. I believe that you came to give us life and that your healing power is just as real today as it was when you walked the earth. Shower them with your grace, Lord. Free them from affliction, bring strength to their bodies and minds, and restore them to health. Come in power, Lord Jesus! Amen. —BF

For Healing of Oneself

O Great Physician, in you I put my trust, not in physicians or in their prescriptions. I do not reject their remedies, but unless you restore the crumbling house of my body, they all labor in vain that build it up. If medicines and therapies are suggested, give them strength to take effect. If not, work patience in my soul, for that is the most certain and most present remedy against all diseases and ills. O Great Physician, in you I put my trust. Amen.

For a Very Sick Child

Almighty God and merciful Father, with eyes of mercy look down upon this sick child. Deliver him (or her) from his bodily pain and save his soul for your mercy's sake. Prolong his days on earth, so that he may be an instrument of your glory by serving you faithfully and doing good in his generation. We ask this in the name of your Son, our Lord Jesus Christ. Amen.

For the Dying

Lord, I lift up to you all those at death's door right now, especially those I may know. Comfort them in their last hours and give them hope in the glory that awaits them. Soften those whose hearts have been closed to you. Show them the reality of your mercy and let them realize that it is never too late to call to you. Help them to forgive all those who have wronged them and to accept your forgiveness for the mistakes they have made. May they be reconciled to you, and feel your loving embrace welcoming them into the joy of eternal life. Amen. —BF

For Someone Who Is Dying

Lord Jesus, by your victory over death and the infinite merits of your passion, we ask, on behalf of this, your servant, that he (or she) may have thoughts of peace, mercy, and comfort. Bear him up against all distrust and despair, deliver him from earthy cares, and be his comforter in his distress. Let those hands, once nailed to the cross, now plead for him and, obtaining his pardon, conduct him into your eternal rest. Amen.

For When I Am Near Death

Receive me, O Jesus, in your loving arms, into which I throw myself as I behold them stretched out for me upon the cross. Receive me to your embraces, which I long for, and draw my soul to yourself. Receive me, O good Jesus, in your mercy. Receive my spirit in peace. Amen.

Jesus, Mary, and Joseph, I give you my heart and my soul. Amen.

For the Souls in Purgatory

Lord, we know that only the pure and holy can stand in your presence. Ease the suffering of the holy souls in purgatory, as you make them ready to meet you. Father, free them from the bonds of their sins and let them see your face at last, as you welcome them into your glorious kingdom. Amen. —BF

For People Who Are Traveling

Lord, be the companion and protector of all our brothers and sisters who are traveling.

Safely bring back to their beloved homes those who have set out on a journey or pilgrimage, so that, giving thanks for your benefits and mercy, they may desire to be fellow citizens with the saints and dwell in your house, forever. Amen.

For Engaged Couples

Father, we thank you for bringing us together, and we ask your blessing on us as we prepare for marriage. Help us to be fully aware of the commitment we are about to make: to give ourselves completely to one another, to be faithful to each other always, and to sanctify one another in the grace of your Holy Spirit. Open our hearts to the gift of children, and let us welcome them joyfully. Above all, during this time, lead us to greater trust in your merciful love and providential care. May we grow closer to you, and learn to put you first in everything. Amen. —BF

For Married Couples

Father, you intended matrimony to be a reflection of your unending love for humankind and your covenant promise to remain faithful to us. Help us to stay true to that intention by always putting you at the center of our marriage. May we call upon you to help us: to always look to the needs of our spouse before our own; to communicate openly and honestly with each other in all circumstances; and to be as ready to forgive our spouse's failings as you are to forgive ours. By the power of your Holy Spirit, renew our love, so our hearts will never grow indifferent to the wonderful blessing we have in one another. Amen. —BF

For a Family and Household

God of goodness and mercy, we commend to your all-powerful protection our home, our family, and all that we possess. Bless us all as you blessed the Holy Family.

O Jesus, our most holy Redeemer, bless us, that we may always openly confess our faith, that we may never falter in our hope, even amid pain and affliction, that we may ever grow in love for you and in charity toward our neighbor. O Jesus, bless us, protect us.

O Mary, mother of grace and mercy, bless us, protect us against evil, lead us by the hand, reconcile us with your Son, commend us to him, that we may be made worthy of his promises.

Bless this house, O God our Father, who created us; O divine Son, who suffered for us on the cross; O Holy Spirit, who sanctified us in baptism. Amen.

For Families

Lord, strengthen our family. Reveal to us any way we may have damaged our relationships. Heal any wound, visible or invisible, that may have brought strife and division into our home. Forgive us for the times we've been cold and apathetic to our loved ones, and give us a new appreciation for each of them. Like your family at Nazareth, may our family also become a school of charity, where we learn above all how to care for each other, and where we teach one another how to grow in kindness, patience, and humility. Amen. —BF

For Me, a Parent, and My Children

O Father, you have given me these children and committed them to my keeping—to bring them up in your kingdom family. Teach me what to give and what to withhold, when to reprove and when to encourage. Help me to be gentle yet firm; considerate and watchful, as I try to lead them, by word and example, in the ways of wisdom and truth, faith and love.

I commend my children unto you. Be their God and Father. Strengthen them as they face temptation and deliver them from evil. Confirm and multiply in them the gifts of the Holy Spirit that they may daily grow in grace and in the knowledge of our Lord, Jesus Christ. Amen.

For Parents

You are the Father of all families: We trust you, Lord, to give us the material means to provide for our children, but we want to give them so much more than food and clothing. May we offer them what they need most from us—our time and our affection. Help us to really be a part of their lives, to listen when they need an ear, encourage when they fall down, and correct when they go astray. Please give us your wisdom and help us to impart your truth to them in all that we say and do. We thank you for the great gift they are to us! Amen. —BF

For Children

Lord, we pray for our children, and for all children, that you surround them with your protection. Send your angels to guard them, and keep them safe from any harm that might come to them. Shield them from anything that would corrupt the precious innocence of their hearts and minds. Let them know the most important thing they can learn: that you love them, and that you have promised never to leave or forsake them. Fill them with your Spirit, so they will grow into men and women who are zealous to serve you alone. Amen. —BF

Chapter 18 | PRAYERS FOR
TWENTY-FIRST CENTURY CONCERNS

For Peace

Lord Jesus, we call on you, the only source of true and lasting peace. Send your Spirit upon all nations that they may learn of you and so come to live in the harmony you intended for them. Break down the barriers caused by ethnic, religious, and political conflicts, and teach all people the way of understanding, cooperation, and forgiveness. May each of us carry your peace within our hearts, and may we always be ready to give it to others. Amen. —BF

For an End to Nuclear Proliferation

Lord Jesus, you have told us that our prayers can move mountains. We ask you to send your Spirit upon the leaders of all nations and move their hearts to stop the dangerous spread of nuclear weapons. Give them the wisdom to look beyond their own borders and seek to safeguard the lives of all people from the horror of nuclear war. May your word be fulfilled, Lord, and may our swords be turned into plowshares! Amen. —BF

For the Conversion of Terrorists

Heavenly Father, we pray that you would open the eyes of all who are bent on committing acts of terror and destruction. Show them that you are not a god of vengeance but of love, and that all life is sacred to you. Reveal to them the truth that you came to save all men, and that your son died to set them free from hatred and unforgiveness. Penetrate the darkness of their minds with your marvelous light, Lord! Amen. —BF

For People Who Are Homeless

Lord, we ask your mercy on the many who have no place to call their home this night. Send your protection to keep them from danger; provide them with food to ease their hunger and shelter to guard them from the elements. Through the charity of others, show them your love and care. Guide them to those who can assist in their search for stable housing and employment. Give them hope for the future and peace in knowing that you are there to suffer with them right now, even in the depths of their misery. Amen. —BF

For the Victims of Sexual Abuse

Lord, we ask that you bring comfort and healing to those scarred and broken by sexual abuse. Free them from any pain, guilt, or shame they may be carrying with them from their past experiences. Show them that they are first of all your children, completely worthy of love and acceptance. Release them from the anger they feel toward their abusers, and bring them to a place of forgiveness. Help them to move on with their lives, Lord, and let them see you as their loving Father, who will never forsake them. Amen. —BF

For the Victims of Natural Disasters

Lord, we ask your special blessing on the multitudes who have suffered the violence and devastation of natural disasters. Reassure them that you are still their comforter and provider, even in the midst of tragedy. Let them never stop trusting in your goodness and mercy! Send them the assistance they are so desperate for; open the hearts of your people to see the tremendous needs of their brothers and sisters and to respond with generosity and compassion. Amen. —BF

For Cures for Cancer, AIDS, and Other Diseases

Father, you gave us the art of medicine to relieve the sickness and suffering of our brothers and sisters. Inspire the medical community with new breakthroughs to cure the scourges of our age: the epidemics of cancer, AIDS, and other terrible diseases that have devastated families, societies, and entire nations. Guide them in using their knowledge and skill to bring miracles of hope and healing to our world. Amen. —BF

For Freedom from Addictions

Lord, you came not just to bring us eternal life, but a new life, free from slavery to sin. I pray for those I know, and for all those who may be addicted to drugs, alcohol, or any substance—or habit—that keeps them in bondage and blocks them from receiving your love. Break their chains, Lord! Through the gift of your grace, let them understand that you are the happiness they seek. By the power of your precious blood, deliver them from the desires that are destroying them. Give them supernatural strength to leave their old life behind and to set their hearts on you! Amen. —BF

ALPHABETICAL LIST OF PRAYERS

F

P

Q

R

S

the WORD among us®
The *Spirit* of Catholic Living

This book was published by The Word Among Us. Since 1981, The Word Among Us has been answering the call of the Second Vatican Council to help Catholic laypeople encounter Christ in the Scriptures.

The name of our company comes from the prologue to the Gospel of John and reflects the vision and purpose of all of our publications: to be an instrument of the Spirit, whose desire is to manifest Jesus' presence in and to the children of God. In this way, we hope to contribute to the Church's ongoing mission of proclaiming the gospel to the world so that all people would know the love and mercy of our Lord and grow ever more deeply in love with him.

Our monthly devotional magazine, *The Word Among Us*, features meditations on the daily and Sunday Mass readings, and currently reaches more than one million Catholics in North America and another half million Catholics in one hundred countries around the world. Our book division, The Word Among Us Press, publishes numerous books, Bible studies, and pamphlets that help Catholics grow in their faith.

To learn more about who we are and what we publish, log on to our website at www.wau.org. There you will find a variety of Catholic resources that will help you grow in your faith.

Embrace His Word, Listen to God . . .

wau.org